THE ADVENTURES AND TIMES OF WILLIAM H. COX II "BILLY THE KID"

WILLIAM H. COX II

IUNIVERSE, INC.
NEW YORK   BLOOMINGTON

The Adventures and Times of William H. Cox II "Billy The Kid"

iUniverse books may be ordered through booksellers or by contacting:

iUniverse
1663 Liberty Drive
Bloomington, IN 47403
www.iuniverse.com
1-800-Authors (1-800-288-4677)

Because of the dynamic nature of the Internet, any Web addresses or links contained in this book may have changed since publication and may no longer be valid.

ISBN: 978-1-4502-4787-0 (sc)
ISBN: 978-1-4502-4788-7 (ebk)

Printed in the United States of America

iUniverse rev. date: 7/23/2010

Introduction

This is a true story and doesn't need any hype or sensationalism to make it interesting. It's about a boy that was born in the mid 1960's and experiences many triumphs and hardships throughout his coming years. In July of 1980 a horrific experience would befall young William at the tender age of thirteen. With the help of his friends and family he managed to pull through this ordeal. Unknowingly a great adventure awaited Billy. He is later taken for a world-wind ride that leads to him becoming a part of American History.

Front Cover Photo: William H. Cox II with ghost of William H. Bonney "Billy the Kid".

Credits

Valdosta Daily Times "Valdosta's Billy The Kid". A special thank you to Dean Poling.

© Morgan Creek Productions, Inc. Illustration in Young Guns DVD Insert.

Billy The Kid Outlaw Gang Photo Credits. A special thank you to Lucas Speer and the rest of the BTKOG.

Herald-Advocate Publishing Company, Inc. "Billy Cox Enjoyed Looking Like Billy The Kid". A special thank you to Jim Kelly.

New Mexico Magazine "The Kid's Double Blazes New Trail". A special thank you to Carol Kay.

Sierra Vista Herald Daily Newspaper "The Return of Billy The Kid". A special thank you to David Eppele.

The Tucson Citizen "Billy The Kid Is Alive and Well and Selling Christmas Trees At The Corner of Campbell and Grant". A special thank you to Julie Szekely.

Bob Boze Bell/True West Magazine Photos from "The Illustrated Life & Times of Billy The Kid". A special thank you to Bob Boze Bell.

The Tampa Tribune "You Can't Take The Kid Out Of Billy". A special thank you to Panky Snow and David Nicholson.

Ruidoso News "Lincoln Visitors Say They've Seen A Ghost". A special thank you to Dianne Stallings. A special thank you to free lance writer Richard McCord.

Fort Sumner Municipal Schools. Fort Sumner High School El Zorro Yearbook Photo Credit.

Clovis News Journal "Outlaws To dedicate Marker" and "Billy The Kid?". A special thank you to Don Cooper.

Guadalupe County Communicator/Santa Rosa News "Billy The Kid Reincarnated" "Billy The Kid Claims District 8 As His Home" Photo Credit: Billy The Kid Outlaw Gang Puerto De Luna. A special thank you to David Delgado.

New Mexico Tourism Department Photo Credit. A special thank you to Mike Pitel.

Fairmont Sentinel "Fairmont GI Pedals 1,300 Miles in 10 Days" A special thank you to Claude N. Swanson.

Bonny Celine Section of Transcript Interview. A special thank you to Bonny Celine.

The Mid Week "Cox Reaches Semifinals, but that's the end of Bartow" A special thank you to Terry Stinson.

The Tampa Tribune "Bartow Boy Reaches Welsh Tennis Finals.

Claude Collins, son of Sue and
Joseph Collins

Ester Gladys Collins, daughter of Sue and
Joseph Collins

The Cox family came from the regions of England, Scotland and Ireland and later settled in North America. Billy's grandmother Jean Marie Collins was born in Versailles, MO and his grandfather Wesley Cox was born in Butler, MO. Billy's grandparents met and fell in love during the depression in Missouri. In the early 1930's they married and later migrated north to Minnesota. There they raised three children named William Hope, Jean Marie and John Cox. There were several members of the Collins-Cox family who partook in some of history's greatest battles such as the Civil War and World Wars I and II. Although they suffered loss and hardship, the family took great honor in serving their country during early America. Billy's grandfather earned his living as a local barber. Barbering was a family trade. Both his father and brother were barbers in Kansas City. Billy's grandmother owned and operated a small family eatery which they named the Ozark Grill. Running the restaurant was very stressful for Jean Marie. Since they were in the middle of a depression she feared no one would be able to afford to eat there. She mainly cooked for the workers building the nearby bridges and dams. Wesley left barbering for a while to help Jean Marie in the kitchen. However, Wesley's father Calvin needed him to come back to work in his shop, so Wesley's time at the eatery became very limited. Wesley received word from his family that Fairmont was in need of a good barber so he decided to move his family there in search of better money.

1

Wesley Hope Cox at the Ozark Grill in Missouri

Wesley Hope Cox

Jean Marie Collins

The price of a hair cut was about twenty-five cents. Wesley was the first to make the transition and later sent for his wife and children. He soon discovered that the pay did not improve. The family completed their move just in time for a horrendous snow storm that blanketed the town. Wesley decided to put his son William to work in the barber shop shining shoes. Later as William began his high school years his younger brother John joined him in the barber shop shinning shoes as well. Wesley felt this would build character for his boys. William and John were the best of friends and would always look out for their sister Jean. A popular hang out for the boys was Mankato River just outside of town. The surrounding lakes made great fishing holes. Fox and Budd Lakes were also their favorite spots. They enjoyed climbing trees in Nelson Park. William especially loved climbing the biggest trees even after he fell out of one of them. Looking to add extra income to the family pocket, John took on a job at a local restaurant and candy shop after school. The rest of the family spent time working on a small farm. Wesley and Jean Marie wanted a good life for their children. Odd jobs in their spare time was a good way to pull in extra cash. The family would go down to the nearby gravel pit to gather rocks needed to build walls.

Jean Marie and William Cox

Wesley Hope Cox fishing in
the Ozarks

There was an accident with Wesley's wife Jean while at the pit one day. She had slipped on a
pile of crushed rocks and almost fell into the river. Everyone became extremely cautious after
that incident. Another way Wesley kept food on the table was to hunt for deer and to go fishing.
His time was well spent because his kill was always plentiful.

Above: Bedo Collins second on bottom left during WWI

Although it would seem the time to work was never end-ing, Wesley and Jean Marie would find ways to be lively and playful with their children. One Halloween Wesley played a simple yet effective prank on his three children. He took a thick piece of string and wrapped it once around a nail and pulled it back and forth which made their house sound as if it way falling apart. He really got a kick from seeing the look on their faces. Susan B. Collins was mother to Jean Marie. She would tell her daughter stories of how she would have to walk along side of cov-ered wagons in travel at the young age of 14. Susan later married Joseph Collins in the late 1800's. The couple was forced to move frequently due to Joseph's unsuccessful attempts in farming. Frustrated with his failures, Joseph abandoned his family. Without Joseph the family suffered many hard times. Several years later he made an attempt to mend his indiscretions but was turned away by the hard-ened Susan. Several years past by and finally Joseph was able to put his life back together with his families.

Jean Marie and her family

Bedo Collins, grandfather of
William Cox Sr.

Members of the Collins Family

Joseph managed to save several thousand dollars to help bring the family back on their feet. Other family members Bedo, Ralph and Olive Collins also lived in nearby Minnesota. Olive's family name was Wolhheater. The Wolhheater's were an important family in Fairmont, MN. The family owned a large three story mansion. On the second floor was a grand dance hall. Some of the finest dancers woud visit the hall from time to time. One night after a dance was held, one of the family members had allowed themselves to become very intoxicated and embarressed the family by riding up and down the streets with a large butcher knife in hand while shouting and swearing. The townspeople had a good laugh and the story was enhanced throughout the years. Wesley and Jean Marie enjoyed watching their children grow and mature. The couples oldest son William married his wife Mary Ellen Stalvey in 1961. Not much is known about Mary Ellen. The Stalvey family came from Georgia and then moved to northern Florida around the Mayo-Bradford area in the 1950's.

Bedo Collins as a child

Bedo Collins in later years

Wesley Hope, Jean Marie and friends during the great snow storm.

Wesley Hope Cox during a great winter storm in 1935

Wesley Hope Cox during the great winter storm of the 1930's

Above: William Hope Cox and his immediate family

William Hope Cox in the Boy Scouts

Above: Bill, John and Jean Marie

Right: Young Bill Sr., John W. and Jean Marie

William and John Cox

Above: Young William Cox

William Cox holding up his catch

Fairmont GI Pedals 1,300 Miles in 10 Days

By CLAUDE N. SWANSON
Sentinel Editor

An English style bicycle,
Release from army duty on completion of service,
A couple of blankets, toilet articles;
A 23-year-old young man.

—o—

Turned loose, and chances are there's material for a story — even if the English style bicycle was made in Holland and acquired, new, for only $40 in cash.

The 23-year-old young man is William Cox, late of the Army Chemical Center, Edgewood, Md., the son of Mr. and Mrs. Hope Cox of Fairmont.

Released on completion of his tour of duty, Cox mounted his bicycle at Edgewood, Md. 10 days and 1,300 miles later, he was at his parents' home, 926 Redwood Drive.

"It was fun," he admitted, "but I don't think I'd do it again — unless, I had a buddy to make the trip with me. It's a good way to see the country, and the trip took 15 pounds off me."

Cox said he averaged better than 100 miles daily.

"The first two days were a bit rough," he said, "but after that, it became routine and I enjoyed it. I found the right speed to trav-

Commissioners OK Girl Scout Camp Site Deeds

Martin county commissioners put finishing touches to deeds yesterday transferring about four acres of land on Iowa lake for Martin county girl scout activities.

Commissioners passed a resolution to accept the land as a gift should it ever revert to the county under the deed's special reversion clause.

The clause states that should the girl scout organization cease to function or use the property, the land will not be sold but revert back to the county for public park purposes.

The deeds were from Mr. and Mrs. Lyle Barker and Mr. and Mrs. Rollo D. Conklin, owners of the two lots. The lots have a combined total of 800 feet of shoreline.

Both parties lowered their price for the land and had necessary papers drawn up when it was learned the Girl Scout organization was interested in the land. Barkers set their price at $1 and Conklins asked $1,000.

In other action yesterday commissioners passed a concurrence resolution to let part of the lands from Blue Earth county school district 83 into Martin county district 77 near Truman.

Commissioners also approved a contractor's request to sublet open work on County Ditch 69 and made preliminary arrangements to appoint some member of the county attorney's office as county civil defense director.

el which tired me the least, and it didn't bother me a bit after that."

Once he was invited to "hitch hike" by grabbing a chain dangling from a truck, and coasting. "I appreciated that, because it was in the mountains, in Pennsylvania. The hill was four miles up, four miles down."

The only other time he got a lift was at Welcome, where a man with a station wagon invited him to climb aboard for the ride to Fairmont.

Expenses were light, probably setting a record for a 1,300 mile cross country trip.

"I spent about $2 a day for food," said Cox. At night, I usually looked for a baseball park, and slept there, wrapped in my blankets. In case of rain, I had a roof over my head.

WILLIAM COX
Peddling Home

I was usually on the road at 8:30 or 9 o'clock in the morning, and I usually put up for the night at 8:30 or 9."

The most beautiful scenery, Cox said, was in Ohio. "I saw a lot of nice, wide streams there. The fruit farms in Pennsylvania also were beautiful. The scenery through Illinois, Indiana and Iowa had a 'sameness' about it that left no particular impression."

Cox entered Minnesota north of Okoboji, and from there he went to Jackson. After that, he took the graveled roads to Welcome.

"Why did you do that?" he was asked.

He blushed, sheepishly.

"I didn't want anbody to see me. I didn't want any publicity."

Then he chuckled: "And here you are, camera and all."

After a week or so at home, Cox will go to Minneapolis to look for a job. A college degree man in chemistry, he hopes to find a job in some laboratory.

Having completed six months in the army, his military obligation will be confined to 5½ years' service in the national guard. That over, his military obligation will be fully discharged.

2 Fairmonters to Attend State Heart Workshop

Mrs. Oliver Anderson and Mrs. Richard Fancher of Fairmont, will attend the third annual Heart council workshop tomorrow and Saturday in Minneapolis.

The workshop is being sponsored by the Minnesota Heart association.

Mrs. Fancher who was county chairman for the group said a council will be established in Fairmont soon. The council serves as a public information group.

Article by Claude Swanson of William Cox biking through three states to get to his home.

16

William on his bike journey

Mary did not face an easy life growing up. She and her younger brother George Jr. Were placed in a foster home at a younger age by their mother who caved under the pressure of raising them. Mary Ellen was a very strong individual. She practically raised her little brother. At the age of eighteen Mary Ellen went out on her own and decided to attend Blue Mountain College in Mississippi for a couple of years then continued her education at the University of Florida where she met William. They had their first child in 1963 while in Minnesota; a beautiful baby girl whom they named Allison. Back in Florida in the year 1966 they welcomed their second child whom they proudly named William Hope II. Finally while in Atlanta, GA in the year 1970 there was another delightful addition to their warm family; another baby boy whom they named John Allen. Mary Ellen later suffered a grave loss in 1975 with the death of her father George Fletcher Stalvey. He passed while she was visiting him in the nursing home; where he was staying. She and her father had a good relationship. In his younger days George had earned his living as a shoe salesman. Although there was peace between Mary Ellen and her father, the feelings she had towards her mother were very different. The animosity between the two only grew over the years. Although she began to show signs of mood swings and depression, Mary Ellen tried to ignore the tension she was feeling and carried on to raise her family. William and Mary Ellen's oldest son Billy was always full of life and had a very adventurous spirit. The early 1970's was a very enthusiastic time for Billy. He had the tendency to run off and play by himself a lot but would always find a way to have a good time.

Mary Ellen Stalvey

18

Mary Ellen would often take her children to Homasassa Springs and Crystal River where they lived. Billy loved all of the parks and animals around. There were also mazes near by were Billy and John would play hide and seek. Billy's father was employed as a chemist at Florida Power. William Sr. Would often bring his children gifts and knick knacks from his job. He was a very giving and loving father. In her spare time Mary Ellen would take the children to places like Yankeetown, Englis or to Cedar Key where they would go fishing. Billy remembers acquiring one of his favorite possessions in Cedar Key; his captain hat. Mary Ellen had friends from Cuba that lived near there and would often join the family on the island. Billy has memories of his mother praying for our troops in Vietnam with hopes that the government would send some of them home. She would yell at the president when he made a television appearance pleading for the troops to return. Another past time of Billy's was listening to music.

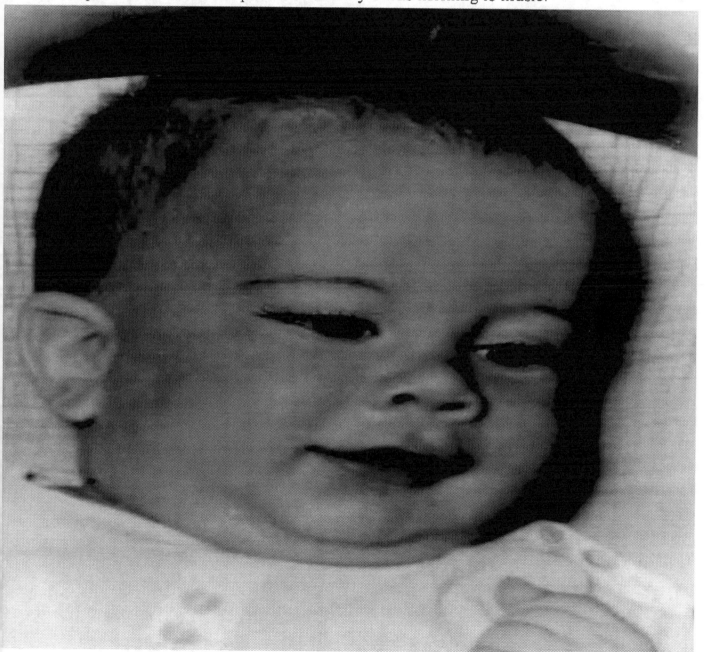

Baby photo of William H. Cox II in Bartow, FL 1966

Some of his favorite artists were James Taylor, The Eagles, Marvin Gaye, Paul Simon, Elton John, Al Green and Santana. As a young boy his favorite song was "Rockin' Chair". He also loved to listen to his mother and sister play the piano for the family. He enjoyed trips to Inverness and Wildwood and going shopping with his mother. There was a grocery store made of rocks located in Yankeetown. Billy once got kicked out of this store. He had a lot of fond memories of his early childhood but, there were also very unpleasant experiences. In 1972 Billy's father went away on business. Mary Ellen was busy taking care of Billy who was feeling very sick. As his mother laid in bed next to her son to comfort him she heard a scratching noise coming from the front door. There were a lot of kids in the neighborhood so she just figured that had to be the source of the racket. Perhaps they were playing with the screened door. However, the more she thought about how late it was the more she dismissed her previous conclusion.

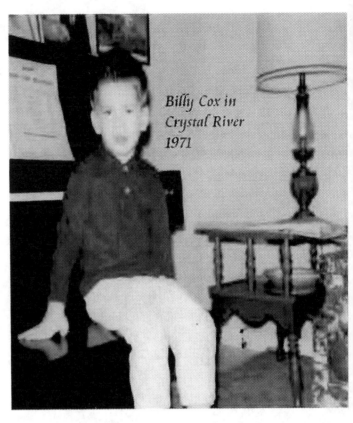

Billy Cox in Crystal River 1971

Allison Marie Cox, 1973

Normally Mary Ellen would shout for her husband to take care of the matter but,because she was alone with the kids she felt it best to stay still and hope the noise would stop. The noise continued for several minutes. Concerned for her children's safety Mary Ellen decided to investigate the scratching. She was hoping it was a small animal; perhaps a stray cat. Billy was told to stay in bed but he watched with wild curiosity as his mother approached the door. When she opened the door there was a strange man wearing a ski mask and holding a knife. She shrieked so loud with fear it woke the entire neighborhood. A terrified Billy shoved his head under a pillow and prayed for the man to go away without harming anyone. On the side of the house there was a second masked invader trying to break in through a window. Luckily Mary Ellen's cry for help scared both men back into the darkness. When William found out about the ordeal Mary Ellen went through he did his best to comfort her. Mary Ellen made the decision to be more cautious when her husband had to got out of town and would think twice before opening her door late at night. Whenever bad things would happen Billy would try to recall his more pleasing memories to sooth his mind. The family would often go to parks for recreation. Billy, Allison and John would enjoy various activities. Billy and Allison once entered an Art contest. Billy happened to be at the park one day when Smokey the Bear visited. He smiled bright for a snapshot with the infamous bear.

Billy with Smokey the Bear in Crystal River, FL 1972

Above: Billy and Allison Cox in Inverness, FL 1972

Billy and Allison Cox in Homassasa Springs 1972

Captain Billy in Sarasota, FL in 1972

Billy Cox in 1972

William Cox II in Sarasota, FL during 1972

Billy once had a life and death experience with a fire. One summer day he and his little brother John were playing in the woods just east of their home. They had decided it would be fun to build a fort. All of the sudden the boys began to smell smoke. John walked up to the road that divided the woods to see where the smoke was coming from. He could see that the woods on the other side had caught fire. John rushed back to Billy to let him know what was happening. Billy thought that their situation was exciting and decided to stay and continue building the fort. The magnitude of the fire was growing larger. John pleaded for Billy to run back to the house with him. Billy refused and continued to play, not understanding the seriousness of the circumstances. With his playful nature Billy threw on an old work hat of his fathers and pretended to be a fireman. He noticed some small flames were getting close to the fort. He threw dirt on the flames to suffocate them. Billy realized that the fire was beginning to surround him. The time for play was over. The smoke began to choke him and his eyes began to water. He would have to think fast to save his own life. About that time he heard fire engine sirens in the distance. He needed an escape plan. Billy scoped out the area around him and noticed a small patch where the flames were weak. He ran with great haste toward the opening and leaped over the flames. After he hit the ground he took off toward the fire trucks. Later he found out that the fire was caused by a cigarette someone had flicked into the woods. In 1972 Billy's father had to go on a business trip to Sarasota but this time decided to take Billy with him.

William Cox Sr. in 1973

Billy was very excited to be traveling with his father. Billy tossed on his captain hat and was ready for another adventure. In fact, he wore his captain hat so often that family and friends started calling him captain. After arriving at their destination Billy and his father rented a room and set off to see the sites. Billy was not used to this type of environment and found it very interesting. There were all kinds of different people walking around. Even the way people talked seemed odd to Billy. There was a mix of various races which Billy thought to be very groovy. He enjoyed watching their facial expressions and listening to the variety of conversations as he passed by on the street.

Mary Ellen, Allison, John and Billy Cox

He noticed that the people walked with a strut in their step. So, he too began walking this way. This made Billy feel very strong and independent even as a child. Later, after Billy and his father returned from the trip, there were family problems waiting for them. Mary Ellen was starting to let the stress of life get to her. Billy remembers his mother starting quite a number of arguments with his father. One evening after supper his mother started a fight with his father over finances. She wasn't happy with her life and was eager to have more money. William asked Mary to stop spending the household income on unnecessary items and put the money toward the bills. Mary Ellen flew into a rage and threw a flower pot at her husband. It landed at his feet and shattered all over the floor. William left the house to cool down and hoped when he returned Mary would have a calmer temper. Young Billy tried to ignore their feuds and hoped they would not last very long. Billy tried to stay positive even under the most stressful of situations.

Mary Ellen Stalvey in 1971

Billy Cox II in 1971

His mother decided to let him take piano lessons, but his attention span would not hold for very long. Billy was a free spirit and although he loved to listen to piano music he would much rather be outdoors playing football with his friends. His sister Allison began taking piano lessons in the early 1970's. Allison played very well. She took her lessons from an older lady who lived in Crystal River. A popular song on the radio at that time was Marvin Gaye's "What's Going On". It was a sad song about a lot of bad things that happened in the 1960's and during the Vietnam War. Billy asked his father if things would get better soon. William assured his son that things would have to improve soon. One of his most favorite outdoor spots was a restaurant located near monkey island in Homosassa Springs. He loved to watch the monkeys come out on their little island and play. Swimming and canoeing was another relaxing past time. He would often go down to the blue hole off of the Rainbow River. He and John like to hike through the woods near the river.

Allison Cox playing the piano in 1972

Billy and John in Crystal River, 1974

Billy liked to make believe that he was living the adventures of Tom Sawyer, just like the movie starring Johhny Whitaker and Jodie Foster. This movie had a big impact on Billy's life. He felt free running up and down the beaches of Sanabel and Cateva Islands. Exploring the island made Billy feel like a pirate in search of treasure. Billy's dad would always take Billy and John treasure hunting with his metal detector. They would often go to some old abandon homes or parks to look for buried coins. Billy was like a bolt of lightning. He once lost a foot race to an older girl that he had a crush on at the island. After the race the girl swooped Billy up in her arms and brought him back to his parents. She told them that they had a fast little kid on their hands. Later Billy enjoyed a beautiful sunset with his parents.

Billy and John in Crystal River, 1972

Billy in Homosassa Springs, 1971

John Allen Cox in Rainbow River, 1974

Right: Little Billy in Cedar Key, 1974

Above: Billy at Sanibal Island, 1974

Lighthouse in Sanibal Island, FL

William Cox in Crystal River, 1974

Billy Cox in Crystal River, 1971

Inverness, FL

Billy loved to watch the television show Bonanza. He would often act out the shooting scenes. He and John loved to play cowboys and Indians together. After playing hard the boys would return home, often to a bon fire their parents where having. They would enjoy hamburgers, bar-b-que and other delicious food. Billy's other favorite television shows included The Rookies, Swat, and The Brady Bunch. He even enjoyed watching the commercials. One particular commercial stood out. It consisted of photos of Jesse James, Butch Cassidy and the Sundance Kid. When the photo of Billy the Kid came on little Billy just turned his head with a sick and scared feeling because he had always heard that Billy the Kid killed hundreds of people. Another thing that bothered him was the photo itself. It was not that great and Billy thought that was the way Billy the Kid himself actually looked. Billy lost interest in that commercial quickly. He would just occupy himself by playing with his toy army men. He like to pretend playing war with them. Billy and John would often wait until everyone else was asleep, then climb out their window to play in the big back yard.

Allison, John and Billy Cox, 1973

Billy especially liked to go outside when there was a full moon. He felt the magic outside seeing the moon light up the sky. The boys would play all night sometimes until they realized it was time to go in before they got caught. Long drives through the country was another passion of Billy's. Often James Taylor would be on the radio. He remembers going to Inverness to visit with his mom's friends and riding to Ocala to visit Six Gun Territory. Billy loved the train rides on the old steam engine and of course the shoot outs on the main street were a blast. He was very enthusiastic about going to the zoos. Billy loved all kinds of animals. His family would often go through small towns. Back then each town usually only had one gas station with two pumps. Billy likes visiting old movies houses where he would see movies like The Apple Dumpling Gang, Butch Cassidy and the Sundance Kid and Tom Sawyer. Billy would make even the simplest of trips fun. Even going to the convenience store would get him excited. He loved to watch all of the different people coming and going. A popular look was wearing bell bottom jeans with high heel boots and leather jackets. Long side burns were also in and made younger people look much older than they were. This wasn't a fashion statement, but just the way people dressed at that time. Billy looked up to the older generation and thought he would never get older. Times were original then. Everything seemed new and exciting.

Billy Cox in Sanibal Island, 1972

It was hard to predict what was coming. Everyday the music was getting better and better. Artists would sing and play from their soul. Even though times were cool, there were also a lot of bad elements such as drug dealings. Marijuana was very common and heroin was becoming a big problem. People in their forty's were passing these drugs down to the youth. Billy remembers hearing about all the drug related crime on the news. Billy's mother and father would help other young people when they could. They would sometimes put up a soldier just coming out of the Vietnam War into a hotel and provide him with a meal and some pocket change when money would permit. Mary Ellen would always give the soldiers a speech on religion while they were in her company. She felt it was her duty to help them find God if they had not done so already. A strange incident happened to Billy and his father while walking along a boardwalk on the river by their house. They ran into and older lady sitting by the water. Billy felt bad for her because she was sitting all alone. He went and sat next to her for a spell to keep her company. She asked him if he came to visit the water. Billy politely answered yes to the woman. She then told him in a firm voice that something special was awaiting him. Billy asked her what it was. She just told him that he would find out in time, but there would be a lot of ups and downs along the way. Billy's father decided to snap a picture of his son with the mysterious lady. Billy decided to go play and run to the end of the pier. When Billy turned around the lady was gone. He tried to find her but she was no where in sight. It had only taken him a couple of minutes to reach the end of the pier and the lady did not have a car near by.

Mysterious Lady at the Pier in Crystal River, 1971

He could not understand how she could have vanished so quickly. He and his father came to the conclusion that she had to have gone into the woods. They never saw her again. That was a very eerie day for captain Billy. During the mid to late 1970's Billy was very active in the Cub Scouts. Billy really enjoyed his time with the group, especially because his father was a scout leader and took the boys to a lot of historical sites in Florida. Billy and his friends from the scouts would walk around old cemeteries to see who could spot the oldest gravestone. If they did not get out before dark things would get a little spooky. One night they came across a fresh grave with the shovel still stuck in the mound. This scared the young boys so they bolted out of the graveyard screaming at the top of their lungs. Billy loved going to places like Disney World, Sea World and Cypress Gardens. He felt free when visiting these places as if he was stuck in time and would never age another day. Another beloved sited for Billy was the historic Bok Tower Gardens

Billy Cox II and his friends in the Cub Scouts at Bok Tower Gardens

He felt a since of magic and history there. When the mid to late 1970's rolled around times where changing. It seemed things were getting better. The music just improved with time. Disco and Funk where getting big. One of Billy's favorite groups was KC and the Sunshine Band. He was also a huge Dallas Cowboys fan. He liked playing football and acting like Drew Pearson, a wide receiver for the Cowboys.

Billy Cox II in Bartow, FL 1976

Billy's mother got him into tennis. Billy spent a lot of time playing these sports and hanging out on the streets. Unfortunately there were still a lot of drugs around. One night just as Billy had left a friends house he heard a voice coming from the darkness. Who ever it was knew his name and called it out. It was pitch dark and very hard to see. As Billy drew closer to the voice he realized it was a neighbor doing heroin. He asked Billy if he had ever tried the drug. Billy firmly replied no and called the neighbor a stupid drug addict. This angered the man and he began chasing Billy all the way home. There was another run in with a drug crowd later on. One day Billy was playing football with some friends and he ran into some older guys who where known drug addicts. They were having a football game

John Allen Cox, 1975 the year the Cox family moved.

of their own. They asked Billy to join them. Billy out ran them all. These guys were between the ages of sixteen and twenty. Billy was only eleven years old. During one play the guys figured the only way to stop Billy was to close line him. Billy's head was jerked back and he fell on his back and neck. This knocked the wind out of Billy. Struggling to breathe Billy gets back up on his feet and begins to cry. He decided to head for home.

Billy Cox II in 1977

Above: Billy Cox II, John, Tony and neighborhood friends

John and Allison Cox at Lake Morton, 1976

The other boys just laughed. That did it for Billy. He was angry and determined not to let them make a joke out of him. He grabbed a sharp stick off the ground and when the guys had their backs turned Billy ran and jumped into the air stabbing the stick into the backs of one of the boys. The injured boy feel to his knees as Billy turned and ran home. After that Billy stayed away from the negative atmosphere and kept close to his friends. His next door neighbor was just like a brother and a super cool guy. Tony, Billy and John would often go swimming together at Lithia Springs or boat down to Wachula in Hardee county. On one trip Tony tilted the canoe over and everyone was dropped into the river. There were moccasin snakes in the water and they were coming fast towards the boys. Tony alerted the others to get to safety. Tony got under the canoe and turned it back up right. After he was in John got in next. They were still waiting for Billy to reach the canoe. After a few minutes all the boys were back in and out of harms way. Billy knew they were all lucky that a gator had not come after them.

Billy, John and Tony in Lithia Springs, 1977

While in Crystal Springs Billy and his friend Jay went across town to play football. They liked to play by the Wonder House. This unique residence was built in 1925 by Conrad Schuck. It featured a natural air conditioning system which used rainwater; outdoor bathtubs on secluded porches; and a system of mirrors which allowed residents to see who was at the front door from any number of locations. This wonderful house was even the topic of a Ripley's "Believe It or Not" cartoon.

Photo from CardCow.com Vintage Post Cards and Collectibles

Billy ran into his tennis buddy Todd while trying to round up some boys to play football with. Todd brought his friend to join the game. Billy recognized Todd's friend from Oak Hill School. His name was Matt. Matt would later become Billy's best friend. Thirteen years down the road Matt would be the one to tell Billy about the movie "Young Guns".

While heading out of town in his family's Plymouth station wagon on another trip to visit some of his mother's religious friends, Billy would often see Tony and his girlfriend Sherry hanging out. Tony and his family were from Immokolee, FL. Tony knew how to fight very well. He took the time to show Billy how to street fight which sometimes meant fighting dirty. Knowing how to fight would come in handy for Billy although he tried to remain cool and collected. He was a real groovy kid. In late 1979 to early 1980 Billy lost his grandfather. He and his father would have to travel to be at the funeral. It was cold and this would be Billy's first time over the road. His father's plan was to take little Billy with him to the airport to fly but there was a problem Billy had a fear of heights and imagined himself falling six

Tony and Sherry in Bartow, FL 1976

miles to his death. So, William Sr. Bought two tickets to ride the Greyhound bus. Coming into Nashville there were a lot of people hanging out on the streets and at the bus station. It was nearly impossible for the two to get any sleep on the bus but they managed to stay somewhat rested.

Lithia Springs, FL

It was crazy in downtown St. Louis. Billy and his father grabbed some lunch at the station. As Billy began to put a spoonful of food in his mouth, he noticed that a man who seemed to be homeless was staring him down. Billy just stared right back at the man who was licking his lips in hope to get some of the food. It seemed to be a staring match between the two. Billy just wanted to eat in peace but feeling bad for the older man he decided to leave some of his food. As his father was paying the check Billy looked back and saw the old man gobbling down what he had left behind.

Cool Billy, John and Allison in Bartow, FL

On his way to Kansas City, MO Billy was able to see the arch which was the gateway to the west. There was a two hour layover in Kansas City. It was late at night and Billy was about to catch a glimpse of the night life. He sat down on a bench by himself to observe the scene. Moments later two beautiful older ladies, one black and one white, came up and sat right next to him. They had beads in their long hair and wore skin tight pants and spiked high heels. It seemed to him that they might be hookers judging by the way they talked and their appearance. They made Billy nervous but that did not stop him from checking them out. A couple of minutes later a black man came strutting up. He wore a fur coat, funky hat and carried a cane. As soon as the man walked by the ladies followed behind him. This man was probably their pimp. Back in those days pimps were real noticeable. A little later Billy saw an old man sleeping on a bench at the station. He watched as a Kansas City police officer walking the beat approached the old man. The officer starting hitting the old man on the foot and shouted for him to get up and go. He told the man to move along because he couldn't sleep there. The old man began cursing at the officer. Billy was amazed at all of the things that went on. He also saw snow for the first time in Iowa as he and his father headed north for Minnesota. It stayed overcast, with snow flurries all the way to Fairmont. After three days of traveling, they finally made it to Albertlea where William's brother came to pick them up to take them to Fairmont. On the way there they all stopped at Perkins for a real home cooked meal. As they got back on their way it was growing colder outside. William Senior and little Billy slept upstairs and got plenty of rest. Morning came and they all had a hearty breakfast together. Billy was excited about seeing his uncle John and his grandma. Billy and his dad had a chance to catch their family up on all that had been happening in their lives down in Florida. Billy was thrilled about exploring the neighborhood so he put on his jacket and headed for the door. As soon as he stepped outside he shouted and jumped back inside the house. The cold up north had a sting to it and Billy wasn't used to that kind of weather. His grandmother gave him her big fur coat to use while he was outdoors. He then set off to explore

Uncle John Wesley Cox in Fairmont, Minnesota 1975

There was a high school a couple of blocks away so he went to check it out. Billy saw two boys playing basketball so he went to join them in the game. Billy was shooting "The Hoop" whom was also a big Magic Johnson and Larry Bird fan. Kids started coming out from the woodwork to hang out at the high school. A girl about fourteen or fifteen years old came to hang out too. The girl asked Billy all kind of silly questions as soon as she found out he was from Florida. She asked him if it got very cold in Florida and if people down there wore jackets. "Of coarse", replied Billy. She then asked him if he had ever heard of the musician named Prince. The name Prince sounded familiar to Billy. She told him that Prince is the biggest musician to ever come out in the music industry and that he was from Minnesota. Billy thought that was very cool. All of the sudden the older boys who were around sixteen or seventeen years old started pushing a car up the street. The girl said that the boys were friends of hers and that they were stealing the car. Billy just decided to let them do their own thing and started to head back to the house for dinner. The next day was the funeral for Billy's grandfather. Billy's dad took his fathers death very hard. It was difficult for young Billy to look over and see his dad cry.

Billy and John, 1975

After the funeral Billy and his cousin Meg walked around downtown Fairmont just talking about life and reminiscing about their grandfather who was a great man. They also talked about the time Meg and her family came down to Florida for a visit. After a week in Minnesota it was time to start heading back home. Billy was thumbing through the yellow pages looking for the number to the nearest Greyhound bus when a hand came smacking down onto the page. It was his dad. He informed Billy that they would be flying home. Billy just put his head down. This was his worst fear coming true. It was very difficult to get him onto the plane. For the first hour of the plane ride Billy kept his head on his father's shoulder. After a while Billy's curiosity got the best of him. He slowly turned to look out the window. All he could think about was how amazing everything looked. He could see everything up above the clouds. He could also see rivers and farmland. This was a truly unique experience. The plane made it's descent to Tampa International airport. It was a very smooth landing. The trip had been a rush but Billy was happy to be home. In the late 1970's Billy was in a play about the Revolutionary War.

Billy Cox II in a play about the Revolutionary War

Billy and his friend Jay were hanging out all around town having fun and living life up. One day while walking home from school the two boys could hear piano music and gospel singing getting louder and louder. As Billy got closer to his house, he realized that it was his mother singing and playing. He would wait for Mary Ellen to stop playing but as soon as she noticed there was an audience she would just turn back to the piano continuing to sing and play even louder. Billy asked Jay if they could go back to his house and hang out with his parents instead. Sometimes Billy's grandmother and uncle would come to visit from Minnesota. Billy's uncle John would send the family pictures that were taken in Minnesota. As the 1970's began to end Billy still continued to play tennis and have fun hanging out with his friends from the Cub Scouts. He would have fun with anything that came his way. His friends were always there for him.

Billy Cox II with his friends in Tampa, FL

In July of 1980 a horrible event would take place for Billy and the family, forever changing their lives. Billy was number one on his junior tennis team which was the best team in their county. They went on to Tampa for the state tournament. They beat Ocala but lost to Tallahassee and Miami which sent them packing back to Polk county. The team was upset but realized they had gone up against fierce competition. Later Billy was invited to eat at the Sam Pam Chinese restaurant in Lakeland by his two friends Mark and Todd. They were all good friends on and off the tennis court. On the way home back to Bartow Billy and his friends were cracking jokes and having a good time. As the car they were in started to near the final turn toward Billy's house everyone stopped laughing. There were hundreds of people standing outside of their homes and lining the streets. There were fire trucks, ambulances and cop cars at Billy's house. In his mind he imagined that his younger brother John had been hit by a car while playing. He had no idea the grim news that awaited him. He finally saw his brother and knew he was alright. As Billy jumped from the car he could hear horrible screams coming from inside his house. John was frantic and crying. He grabbed Billy and told him that their mother had shot herself in the chest. Billy could not believe his ears. The emergency team was working on his mother but she was loosing a lot of blood fast. Billy broke through the crowd and dashed toward the house. He was yelling and pleading at an officer to tell him what was going on. The police officer stopped Billy and escorted him and John to a police car which took them quickly to the police station. There, Billy and John sat with their heads down for what felt like an eternity. They were in total shock but felt very strongly that their mother would pull through. After the boys were interviewed by the local authorities a cab picked them up. The driver had orders to take the boys to the local church music director's house. Billy and John were brought to the basement of the house where there were a lot of church members waiting to offer comfort and support to the boys. Billy's dad had remained at the hospital with the preacher and the music director. By this time it was nine o'clock at night. Billy just paced back and forth. His hands were shaking very badly. He was praying for word that his mother was okay. Billy started asking everyone in the room if they thought his mother would be alright. Everyone tried their very best to comfort and calm him down. The clock struck midnight and Billy could see the headlights of a car shining through the upper window. At this point Billy's patience had worn thin. He had to find out something. The suspense was eating him up. The door slowly opened and the preacher walked down into the basement followed by the music director and then William Sr. Their heads were all down. Billy could see a tear coming from his father's eye. At that moment

Billy got his answer. All of the sudden Billy shouted, "No, please no"! He started knocking things over and darted at the walls and climbing them like some sort of wild unattainable animal. It took five grown men to bring him down. Billy was still punching and swinging at everyone with all his might. Everyone in the room had begun to go crazy. At the tender age of thirteen Billy had suffered one of the most horrendous events a child could go through; the loss of his mother. It was a violent and tragic death.

Billy had no comprehension of how his mother's demise would affect him later in life. He felt his world crumble. His bright and innocent nature had been darkened and damaged by this experience. The first couple of years were rough. He was always getting into fights and getting suspended. Billy would attack anyone and everyone, no matter what the age difference, if they so much as breathed a derogatory remark about his mother. However, as much as it hurt and as hard as it was to go through something like this Billy decided that he would not go down. He would rise, grow and learn from this incident. "That which does not kill us only makes us stronger". This was a phrase he started to believe in. He felt his troubles would only get worse if he did not come to terms with his issues. His friends were a godsend. They all helped Billy pull through the hard times and before he knew it he was back on his trail of fun and adventure. Billy was strong willed and determined to do things his own way. He always told his friends that he would never settle and that he would never be told what to do and how to do it. He was his own person. His dad got remarried a year later. This was rough on his children.

Bill Sr., Billy II and John at Thanksgiving, 1981

Billy was feeling pressured by the rules of the system, so he decided to create his own system. When he got his chance, nothing and no one could touch him. Although his skin was getting thick there were things in life that still got to Billy such as eating at the dinner table without his mother. He missed her presence so much. Billy had dreams of becoming a pro in tennis and touring the state of Florida. Between the pressures of trying to raise his ranking in tennis and the family troubles at home this eventually led to Billy making bad grades at school. Billy's circle of friends grew as the 1980's arrived. He and his friends became notorious for their "oranging" of cars. They would also cruise the city and head out to the beach a lot. Chasing women was also a big thrill. In 1984 Billy was a sophomore. He threw a huge and unforgettable party that year that had the entire school buzzing. He was always known for throwing the best and wildest parties. However, after 1984 some of his friends drifted apart and Billy began to meet new and interesting people.

Captain Billy Cox II, 1984

In 1985 Billy was having too much fun with his friend Matt so he got burned out on tennis and eventually quit the sport. This had been a passion of Billy's for ten years. He had a lot of good times with the sport. He had gone to the tennis academy at Grenelefe and at the University of Florida during the years 1981 and 1982. He had even played with great tennis pros like Jim from Dade City and other greats from the state of Florida. At one time Billy was ranked in the top one hundred tennis players in the state of Florida during the late 1970's and early 1980's.

Billy Cox II just won a tennis tournament in 1982

Cox reaches semifinals, but that's end of Bartow

By TERRY STINSON
Midweek Correspondent

When Bartow High's boys and girls tennis team went to Titusville for the district meet, head coach Harry Burrus was hoping his teams would find some success.

But it didn't happen.

Billy Cox, a sophomore, made it all the way to the semifinals, but that was far as he could get.

Cox got started on the right foot as he drew a bye for the first round, and then in the second round, he won by a default as his opponent, Billy Ray of Auburndale, failed to show.

Cox finally got a chance to show his skills against Scott Infinger of Auburndale. He ripped Infinger in straight sets, 6-2, 6-2, to reach the semifinals against the No. 3 seed in his class, Orlando's John Holt. However, Holt proved to be too much for Cox as he trounced him in two sets, 6-3, 6-1.

"He was too strong for me," Cox said. "He had a high-kicking serve and a lot of top spin."

Holt's high serve kept Cox from returning a good shot and keeping the ball at his opponent's fee, which was Cox' strategy. "He kept me on a defense and was too strong for me," he continued.

Cox was the only Bartow player to score a victory in the boys' tournament, as the Yellow Jackets completed their season.

In the girls' meet, Hope Traxler made the best showing for the Lady Jackets as she made it to the quarterfinals. Traxler bombed Titusville's Krison Goff, 6-2, 6-1. Her next opponent was Lisa Koopman of Titusville Astronaut. Koopman opened up with a 5-1 lead in the first set, but Traxler came back to make it 5-4. Koopman, though, finished Traxler off, 6-4, to win the first set. This seemed to take the winds out of Traxler's sails as she dropped the match by losing the next set, 6-1.

In the No. 1 matches, Bartow's seventh ranked player Teresa Farr had to play in place of absent Julie Carnes. Farr put up a good fight, but was overpowered by Auburndale's Kim Charron, 6-0, 6-1.

(Continued on Page 18)

Above Article by: Terry Stinson

Bartow Boy Reaches Welsh Tennis Finals

Billy Cox of Bartow climbed to the finals, out of 32 international entries, in the Tampa Welsh Tennis Tournament where he finished second in consolation play following two wins and two losses.

Bartowan Mark ████████ advanced to the semi-finals of the tournament.

Cox defeated ████████████ in the boys 16s division, 7-6, 6-4, to advance to the finals.

Article from Tampa Tribune

58

Billy and his friend Matt in North Carolina, 1986

Later that year Billy met another couple of fellows named Junior and Rick. They were brothers that would eventually become close friends of Billy's. John would also hang out with Billy and the boys. On the weekends the boys would make music videos while lip singing to their favorite songs. They would record their moves so that they could watch them later and have a good laugh. The gang also liked to hang out at various clubs in Tampa and Orlando. Junior, Rick and Billy would hang out at Junior's dad's ranch in Fort Meade. The boys would often bring girls out to the Santa Fe Ranch. Although Billy was having a lot of fun in the 1980's he was sad when the 1970's came to an end. One night in 1986 Mike, also known as Snook, and Bubba got Billy to drive with them around Tampa to check out the scene. Before leaving Bartow they wanted to pick up some beer so they drove to the neighborhood convenience store. They parked on the side of the store and Billy got out. He entered the store knowing he was too young to buy the beer. He figured he would try his luck since he happened to know the clerk on shift that night. She decided to take Billy's money which excited him until he noticed a police officer standing to his right on the outside of the store. The officer was checking out Billy's friends. He had to find a way to get he and his friends out of this sticky situation or they and the clerk could get in a heap of trouble. The clerk had not noticed the officer yet. Billy asked her if there was a better brand of beer. She replied yes and Billy said he would go and get it.

Brothers Junior and Rick, 1986

He calmly turned around and headed toward the cooler. When he reached the cooler he told her to forget it because he was not in the mood to drink beer tonight. He grabbed some Dr. Pepper and hoped that she wouldn't be able to put two and two together because of the officer outside. Billy asked that the drinks be bagged. As he headed toward the car his friends had their heads down. They were afraid of getting caught with the beer Billy went in to buy. Billy just played along. He looked at the officer with a surprised look on his face. "Come on over here boy and show me what's in the bag", said the officer to Billy. Billy put his head down as if he was in trouble and walked slowly over to the police officer. "You boys were going to party tonight, huh?" asked the officer. Billy replied yes. The officer told the boys they would not be partying tonight as he reached his hand inside the paper bag. He grabbed a hold of the contents and lifted out a six pack of Dr. Pepper. "Dr. Pepper", shouted the officer. All of the boys started laughing. "You've got to be kidding me", said the officer as he started to laugh. He told the boys they were free to go knowing this would make a funny story to tell his fellow officers. Pleased with his hi jinks, Billy got back into the car and drove off with his friends. That same year Junior and Ricky introduced Billy to a Spanish girl that they both knew. Billy would see her every once in a while when he was in the Ft. Meade area. Junior's father Johnny owned a trucking company hauling produce. The company was based out at the Santa Fe Ranch.

John Cox, 1987

One day Matt came to the ranch to see if Billy wanted to ride to Asheville, North Carolina for a road trip. Brad, Matt, Scott and Billy decided to take the trip. Junior and Ricky had to stay behind and work. The others headed to Maggy Valley, NC They went down to the river and then up the mountain to attempt to ski, however, they did more falling down than anything. They then checked out some old trails and Civil War battle grounds. This was a good time and the history was exciting.

Billy and Matt in North Carolina, 1986

On another night during the late 1980's Junior, Ricky and Billy decided to hit a Lakeland night club at a nice hotel. The dance floor was packed and there were hot women everywhere. After a few drinks everyone was feeling good. Billy was buzzing. Billy and his friends all headed for the bathroom. They all had a few drinks in them, so they were talking and laughing very loud. They didn't realize that there was someone in the stalls. Billy was talking out loud and told his friends that he could not believe he was being served because he was only sixteen years old.

While Billy was washing his hands the man who had been in the stalls came out but did not say anything to him. Back at the lounge Billy asked Ricky if he wanted another drink. Rick said yes and they both walked back up to the bar. When the boys asked the bartender for two more beers he apologized that he could not serve them anymore. He had been informed that Billy was only sixteen years old. Billy had only been kidding about his age. The bartender was not joking. Billy became pissed. He could not remember what the guy looked like that had overheard them in the bathroom. Naturally his buzz did not help. Billy started walking up the bar passing behind the people drinking. After passing behind about twenty people Billy stopped and quickly turned around. Sure enough there was a man at the other end of the bar who was watching Billy. The man quickly snatched his head back straight ahead. Billy had found the guy who reported him. He strolled down the bar toward the man and asked him if he was the one who had told the bartender he was only sixteen years of age. The man nervously answered yes. "Don't be afraid my brother", Billy said to the man. "I just can't believe I caught you. I'm a slick kid, aren't I ?" The man just nodded his head. Billy told the man he would see him later down the road and he and his friends left for another joint.

Billy Cox II partying, 1986

The late 80's became more exciting. A lot of different types of people were close to Billy. He was still working at Maas Brothers. He had a girlfriend named Lea Ann which only lasted about five months, but Billy didn't care because there were a lot of women everywhere to choose from. About this same time frame, Billy met Jose' through some mutual friends. Jose' was from Spain and had come to the United States in the early 70's. His family lived in Manhattan for several years before moving to Florida. Jose' had a lot of respect for the 70's era and so did Billy, which was one of the things that made them good friends. A lot of wild parties went down at Jose's casa. One of the groups main hangout places was T.A. Slammer's and Mons Venus. They also visited a night club pretty often called Sting Rays. The gang was having a blast and staying up all night. Most of the crew, especially Billy, did not care much for the system as long as things could stay simple. They were all happy doing whatever they wanted. On another night Matt, Michelle, Diana, John, Brad and Billy went to the airport to watch the planes and ride the shuttles. They did this until early into the morning and then slept on top of each other in the middle of the airport until security woke them up and asked them to leave. With no place to go and still very tired the gang headed to the beach to get some sleep.

Jose' in Lakeland, 1988

Lea Ann and her child, 1988

After about one hour of resting a loud horn began to blow. Matt's eyes popped open and he saw a large machine with big tires that was cleaning the beach and heading right for them. He leaped to his feet and shouted for everyone to get the hell up and get out of there. They all ran as fast as they could from the beach cleaner. Matt started to throw shells at the machine and the man driving it in hopes to get him to chase them. Billy ran up to Matt and asked him if he was crazy. It was five o'clock in the morning and the cops would be there in a few minutes. Finally they all decided to pile back into Matt's car to get some sleep. Once back in Polk county Billy decided to take a drive to Fort Meade to check on Junior, Ricky and Johnny. On Fridays after work Johnny would get beer and cook steaks and fajitas for everyone. He would always invite Billy to have some food with them. Some other friends of the family, Manual, Franky and Mandeo would come and hang out there. This was Billy's favorite hang out for years to come. Many women would pass through the ranch much because of Junior and Ricky. Billy didn't mind helping himself to some of the action. It was now the summer of 1986 and Billy was nineteen years old and out of school. He was not able to walk with his class at graduation because he was one credit short. All by himself, he had to watch his class walk from across the field. Billy knew he had a tough road ahead and the reward would be much bigger than the diploma. So, he just smiled and walked away.

Billy Cox II going to the prom on a ship in Tampa, 1986

A week later Billy approached his brother John about taking a boating trip out of the crystal river area which was on the ocean. John gathered plenty of food while Billy got his knife and other survival gear together. Of coarse, Billy took along his captain hat which he was known for wearing. The boys came into Crystal River at about eleven o'clock in the morning. They rented a small john boat with one motor. Soon Billy and John were heading out to sea. Since they had no compass Billy figured they could use the smoke stacks from the Crystal River nuclear power plant as a way to see how far out they had gone.

Billy deep in thought while in North Carolina

After a few minutes Billy decided to turn around and see how far they were from the smoke stacks. Unfortunately, he could barely see them. "Oh, god"! Billy thought. Soon the boys became very frightened and started to panic. Billy then turned the boat around and tried to stay on course with the smoke stacks. All of the sudden a thunderstorm fiercely rolled in. Now, because of the rain they could not see anything at all. Billy tried to remain calm and to keep control of the situation that seemed to be turning ugly for him and his brother. He assumed they were heading in the right direction so he continued on course. The rain was pounding hard on the small boat. Billy could see something up ahead and it looked like trees. It wasn't the coastline of Florida. It was an island. Billy pulled the boat up on the shore. He and John grabbed the cooler with the drinks and food in it and looked for cover from the rain. They found trails all over the island. They took parts of palm trees and pieced together a roof to keep them from getting more wet. It rained for about another forty-five minutes. The

Photo from: worldofstock.com

boys were happy that at least they did not have to wait out the storm in the water. Billy thought this was exciting and when he told that to his brother he got the strangest look. After a couple of hours the steam from the rain had cleared up. Billy walked back to the shore line to take a look. He could see the smoke stacks and they appeared to be bigger. This meant that they were closer to the shore line than he had anticipated.

This would lead them back to the river which connected to the marina so they could get back home. The boys loaded back into the boat and tried to start the motor. At first it would not crank, but luckily after a couple of tries it fired up. They smiled at one another, left the island and headed for home. On the way up the river they passed by the owner of the boat rental shop. Since it was late the owner had been out searching for them. He was happy to see that they were alright. As they got closer to their destination John turned to Billy and asked him if he had found anything valuable. Billy just shook his head and said "Yes, I found an adventure". You're crazy", John replied. It was sometime during 1986 and Billy was out of high school and in need of extra money. Billy thought he would try his luck at selling Kirby vacuum cleaners. It seemed fun at first but it was hard selling vacuum cleaners to older people who did not have a lot of money. On one trip out while selling vacuums it had started to get late when his boss asked him to go show a vacuum to a lady who lived in Plant City. When Billy got into town he came into an area that seemed a little rough. He was cautious as he drove down to the apartments where he was to meet the customer. As he pulled into the complex some strange guys were walking out. A lady was waiving at Billy to come over to her apartment. At the same time he looked back at the guys who were now heading over in his direction. The rain was really coming down harder. The lady kept waving her hands in the air in an effort to get Billy to come over. The kid's instincts kicked in and he knew this situation was trouble. It was not hard to put the two situations together and realize it was a setup. Billy threw his car into reverse and then drove off. On the way out he had to pass the strange men. As he went by them going about fifteen miles an hour one of them hit the truck hard causing the car to stall. Billy coasted out of the parking lot and onto the main road which took him back towards the highway. He put the gear into neutral so that he could try to get the car to start while in motion. However, he was having no luck. The car finally came to a stop. All of the sudden a guy came up to Billy's window and told him to get out of the car. In seconds Billy leaned over to the passenger door and got out of the car. He took off running. He was scared that the men might have a gun. He ran through and behind apartment complexes while onlookers just stared. He headed north until he saw a church up ahead in the distance. He figured there might be help for him there. As he came upon the door he burst inside and interrupted the sermon that was going on. By the color of Billy's skin he stood out like a sore thumb. Everyone turned around at the same time and stared at him. He just quietly walked in and sat down so that the pastor could finish his sermon. The pastor came up to Billy and asked him if everything was ok. Billy told him that he almost got robbed down the street while trying to sell Kirby vacuum cleaners. The pastor asked Billy if he knew the Lord. The kid replied "Yes, I do". The pastor said that people die everyday in circumstances like this all over the country, but told Billy that this was not his day to die. The pastor called the sheriff and then took Billy to his car. The robbers could not get to the vacuum because it was locked in the trunk, which was a good thing. The sheriff and the pastor helped to jump off Billy's car so that he could go home. In the summer of 1987 Billy took to the road by himself for the first time. He was twenty years old now and looking for another crazy adventure. A magazine company had hired him to travel the United States as a sales rep. Billy had a good time selling magazines in north Florida, Alabama, Arkansas and Mississippi. Once he got picked up in a little town by the police chief for soliciting which resulted in a nice fine in exchange for his release. He ran into other boys that had trouble while selling the magazines.

Billy and a good friend of his named Chuck from North Carolina borrowed a car in Mississippi to go to a bar to meet some older women. Chuck decided to drive that night. They were pulled over for speeding. The officer walked up to Chuck and asked for his driver's license. The problem was that he did not have one. The officer became suspicious and started shining his flashlight in the back seat to look around. Chuck asked the officer if he had a search warrant for looking in the car. Billy knew that was the wrong thing to say to a Mississippi cop. He was so scared by the situation that he felt he would wet himself. Back up arrived to assist the officer. Some of the cops started pointing at Billy and told him to get out of the car. However, form Billy's demeanor they could tell that he was respectful of the law. He was not giving the officers any trouble so they let him go. As one of the cops threw Chuck into the police car he yelled to Billy "You saw what that cop just did, right"? The other officers looked at Billy, waiting to see what he was going to say. "I didn't see a damn thing", said Billy. Then he slowly walked back over to the car and drove away. After about two months of selling magazines Billy grew tired of the craziness. Billy and another guy were dropped off at a truck stop about thirty miles west of Benton, Arkansas. It was the middle of the night. The other guys' name was Marcos. He was upset about being dropped off in the middle of the night. Billy on the other hand was thrilled. He loved the challenge. He had acquired a long list of names and numbers from people he had tried to sell magazines to. Billy had a charming way about him.

This is the spot in Arkansas where Billy and his friend had
to camp out after being fired from the magazine company

Billy had lived in Benton for a little while. He soon met a young fellow named Jimmy. Jimmy introduced Billy to his father, Jim Senior, who had a family owned roofing business. Shortly after meeting Billy, Jim offered him a job. The pay was good, but the work was very hard. Billy had to carry his shingles up the ladder in the heat which could be very exhausting. Once Billy, Jimmy, Jim Senior and another son Tony were in Pine Bluff on a job site. The house they were working on was old and had a steep roof. As Jimmy took the old shingles off with a shovel Billy would throw them into the back of their truck. The roof was so steep that Billy started to fall. He grabbed hold of some shingles and started sliding down the roof.

Neighborhood where Billy lived for 5 months in Benton, Arkansas

Just as he was about to slide off the side of the house, Jimmy reached to him the end of the shovel so that Billy could grab hold. As nails and other debris fell beneath him, Billy looked down at the drop he faced and then back up at Jimmy. This was a close call for Billy. Jimmy started laughing and pulled him back up to safety. Jimmy and Billy became very close friends. They were always cruising around Benton looking for girls and meeting Jimmy's other friends. One of Jimmy's friends named Emmett liked to go snake hunting down the river. Billy was not to crazy about Emmett's hobby so he opted not to go. Instead he met up with some other friends who took him to church. There he met a lot of good people. There was a lot of talk about their governor Bill Clinton. He always head good things about Mr. Clinton. The locals would always tell Billy that Arkansas could put a wall around their state and support themselves without any outside help.

Jimmy Senior who owned a family roofing company

He discovered a lot of history in the town. He was told that once Jesse James had his cave near by. Billy stayed in Benton for six months, just living life up and saving as much money as he could. He remembers having strange feelings when he would see the sun set in the west. He would stare at the sunset and wish he could go out west and explore something incredible. He thought that maybe something was out there just waiting and possibly searching for him. But, he figured it all to be a dream. Billy started getting homesick. He missed his family and friends. He bought a trailway bus ticket back to Florida. He said goodbye to everyone and told them that he would write soon. His friends Phil, Linda and Richard told him to always follow his dreams. Jimmy shook Billy's hand and told him that it was good knowing him. He asked him to look him up if he ever made it back that way. "I sure will brother", said Billy as he jumped onto the bus. Finally, Billy was back in Polk county. He rounded up his old gang and continued having a great time. Matt had got Billy a job at Maas Brothers which was a clothing store and up scale restaurant in Lakeland. Here, Billy was busing tables. Matt worked in the china department while their other friends worked on the dock. This was a fun job for Billy. Junior and Ricky would come pick Billy up and take him to some Hispanic night clubs in Fort Meade, Wachula, Bowling Green and Arcadia. Johnny and his brothers Amando, Franky and Manuel had their own Tejano band. Billy really got into the music they played. Matt invited Billy to go to the movies with some friends of theirs. He asked Matt what the name of the movie was. Matt told Billy "Young Guns". He did not tell Billy what the move was about but said that he should like it. During this movie Billy felt intrigued by the landscape. There were also foothills and small rivers with brush along the side. There also adobe homes with wooden logs at the top. It was the story line that gave Billy hard core chills from his head to his toes. Matt tried to get Billy's attention but his eyes were glued to the screen. "Did this really happen", Billy asked Matt. "Yeah, I guess so", said Matt. "I just have to go see these places in New Mexico, said Billy. I wonder if they're still out there". The places he was referring to were Lincoln, Fort Sumner, Roswell and other surrounding areas. Later at home Billy pulled out his map and looked up New Mexico. First he found Roswell and noticed that Lincoln, Capitan and Fort Sumner where close by. He just couldn't believe that these events actually happened there. He made up his mind to check it out. Just before going out west Matt asked Billy to go with him to New Orleans for two weeks and hang out on Bourbon Street. While in the French quarters Matt and Billy partied hard. This area had some of the best jazz bars around. They wandered the streets until four in the morning and looked for wild women. Matt asked Billy if he was really going to New Mexico. Billy replied "Yes, I have to go. You only live once and I want to live it to the ultimate". Matt supported Billy and thought what he was going to do was very cool. Days later Billy and Matt went shopping on Canal St. They came across a unique hat shop. Billy spotted an awesome stove pipe hat. He told Matt he had to have this hat to take with him on his trip to New Mexico. So, he paid for the hat and happily wore it all around the French quarters. As a joke he even proudly posed for a picture in his new hat on Bourbon Street as the town drunk.

Billy Cox II imitating the famous pose of the town drunk on Bourbon St.

After acting crazy in New Orleans and dealing with some minor car trouble, Billy and Matt headed back east to Florida. It was now the summer of 1989. Billy had some vacation time coming up, so he packed his bags and jumped on a bus heading west, passing through Alabama, Mississippi, Louisiana, the big state of Texas and finally ending in Roswell, NM.

New Mexico State Flag

He was twenty two years old now and full of energy. Billy stepped off the bus, not knowing where to go. He just went with the direction of the wind. It led him in the direction of the Roswell Museum. When Billy walked through the doors a fellow named Ken, who was a historian there, approached Billy. Ken told him that he looked just like "Billy the Kid". "What's your name", asked Ken. "Billy" replied the kid. Ken's mouth dropped open. He told Billy that he needed to get him to Lincoln, which was only about sixty miles from Roswell.

Ken and his family in Lincoln, NM 1990

A few days later Billy prepared for the ride of his life; an experience that would change him forever. Ken's family took Billy in and gave him odd jobs. Billy became very fond of the family. Ken had lived in Roswell for twenty-five years but, was originally from Indiana. Billy became very good friends with Ken's son Shannon and his friend Todd. Sometimes the three boys would go from bottomless lakes to the Hondo river just outside Chaves county toward Lincoln county. They would all ride the crossing which would take them over the Hondo River. One time while doing this Todd was stung several times by hornets so they had to shorten their trip and head back to Roswell. Ken told the boys that he wanted to take Billy to the mountain near Cloud Croft and camp out and then go over to the foothills surrounding the little village of Lincoln. Ken welcomed them to ride along. Billy was amazed at the scenery he saw on their way to Lincoln.

"The Kid" in downtown Lincoln, NM 1990

They stopped in San Patricio to get some water for the high county. Then they finally made it to Sunspot near Cloud Croft where they made camp. The local ranger warned them that bears were bad this year and cautioned them to keep food out of their tents. Ken and the boys went to explore the mountains while Ken's wife Donna prepared the food. Later after dinner they sat around the campfire listening to Ken play the guitar as they all sang. Tired and full of food everyone decided to get some shut eye. In the middle of the night Billy thought he heard a noise so he got up to investigate. Sure enough there was a bear rummaging through the trash. Billy remained quiet and the bear finally left the scene. The next day Billy told everyone what he saw. After a couple of days of sunspot everyone packed up and started heading towards Lincoln. Billy was falling more and more in love with the land. He confided to Ken that he felt as though he had been to this land before. On their way into the town of Lincoln they passed by a very old cemetery on the right which was fascinating to see. Ken drove into the center of town and parked the truck in front of John Tunstall's store. They all decided to head west towards the old courthouse. Ken got Jack, who was the chief ranger in Lincoln, and introduced him to Billy. When Billy stepped foot onto the courthouse porch, Jack looked as though he seen a ghost. While Billy explored the courthouse Jack followed behind taking photos of him. A new "Kid" was born. Jack invited Billy to stay in Lincoln and promised there would be work for him.

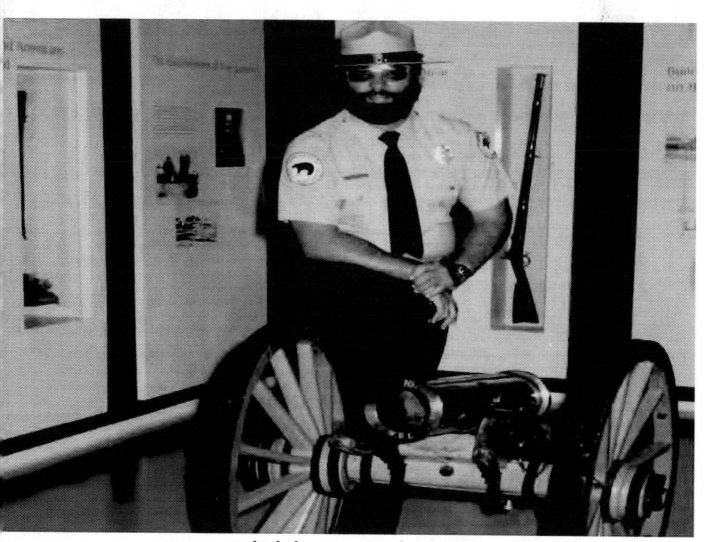

Jack, Chief Ranger in Lincoln County, 1989

Lincoln, New Mexico in the 1980's

Ken and his family set up camp just outside of Lincoln. Everyone enjoyed playing along the Rio Bonito. Later that night there was good food and music followed by plenty of rest. Later, Billy decided to go back to Roswell with Ken and his family. A few weeks later they had a party out at the park near the base. This is were Billy met Tom, who was married to Ken's daughter. Tom spoke with Billy about the land surrounding Lincoln and said he knew it very well. After the party was over Billy and Tom planned to go back into Lincoln county.

The two met up with Manny who was also friends with Jack. Then the group introduced Billy to Joe and Harvey over at the general store, which was one of their hang outs. Before long Billy was known all over the town. Jack informed Billy that there would be a big fiesta going on at Cedar Creek over the weekend. So, when the weekend came Billy headed to the fiesta.

Above: Jack in early New Mexico days during the early 1970's

The General Store in Lincoln, NM. This is the only place to get food. On the left is Joe S. His grandfather rode with Billy the Kid. On the right is Harvey D. He is the owner of the store.

Billy the Kid Outlaw Gang Fiesta

There were a lot of people there from all over the state. Billy met Joe and his wife Marilyn who were throwing the party. Joe and Marilyn were from Taiban. Joe was a big politician from Santa Fe and used to work with the governor of New Mexico. During the 1950's and 1960's he owned a lot of gas stations along Route 66. The couple told Billy to drink up, eat hearty and have a good time. Manny and Billy went to get a bowl of posole which was a Mexican soup consisting of pork and garbanzo beans with a tomato base. It was usually eaten with flour tortillas. Loretta made the best posole. The kids had potato sack races and played hide and seek. Joe and his wife Colleen rode in from Salazar canyon just west of Lincoln. Lacy who was Joe and Colleen's daughter played the guitar while her sister Dora sang. Billy danced and played along with the kids. Scott, Blake, Patrick, Darush and Kevin who where from Lincoln came to the celebration too. Billy met James who came to El Capitan, New Mexico from Texas years ago. James was in politics and is now the current sheriff of Lincoln county. Carrizozo was the county seat of Lincoln county. James would stay busy chasing the usual outlaws. This would vary from drug smuggling, to cattle rustling or finding people who got lost in the mountains.

The Kid shaving in Ruidoso, NM, 1990

Sometimes he had to go fetch some drunks that were causing trouble in the White Oaks Saloon. White Oaks, NM was a very happening place. It was know for it's wild dances.

White Oaks Saloon, 1990

James would tell everyone to put their troubles aside and have a good time at the dances. James shook Billy's hand and officially welcomed him to Lincoln county. A Spanish lady approached Billy. She took off a brown necklace that she was wearing and placed it around Billy's neck while saying "Welcome back Billy, you've come back to us". Billy looked down with a serious look on his face. Time returned to normal after the big fiesta was over. Manny and Billy rode in early to Lincoln up to Tunstall's Store where Manny worked. Manny was also a state ranger. Part of his job was to protect the store and give visitors insight to it's history. Manny always proclaimed that one day "The Kid' would come and visit the store.

The real sheriff of Lincoln county, James M. Right: Billy Cox "The Kid"

Above: Ranger Manny at Tunstall's Store

Manny working in Tunstall's Store

One day Billy was at the store when Kevin informed him that Jack needed a word. So they both met up with Jack at the courthouse. Jack pitched an idea to Billy for the two of them to do a gig together at the courthouse. Billy would be paid a percentage of the proceeds collected from donations. Billy accepted the partnership. Jack would tell the story of "The Kid's" famous escape in 1880 to the tourists. Following the story Jack would ask the audience if they believed in ghosts. Then William Cox II, Billy, would walk in with a Winchester in his hand while wearing a stove pipe hat and sweater. He would also strike Bonney's famous pose. Kids began to cry and the older people started grabbing at their chests. Billy then turned and strutted out of the room. People gave Billy a good amount of money. The state of New Mexico also profited nicely from the show. Tourists approached Billy on the street asking to pose in pictures with him. He happily obliged. Before long, he was know as the "Modern Day Billy the Kid". Later that evening Jack, Billy Kevin and Manny went over to Kevin's mother's house for dinner. Kevin's mother Sharon and her father Jake were good people. She made a great casserole and a pitcher of sweet tea. It was delicious. After dinner Jake would tell stories of when he was a young buck working cattle from Lincoln county to Roswell. He had lived in Lincoln since the 1930's. Times were very different but Lincoln still remained the same. One day Dustin, John a friend of John's and Jack's dog Moakie would hike the trail behind Jack's house that led on top of the foothills.

Billy and Moakie in Lincoln, NM 1990

Sharon who was a ranger and her father Jake at Tunstall's Store

The terrain gradually became flat again and they would hike until they found the old San Patricio, Ft. Stanton Trail. Dustin and John had been on this trail several times and had wanted Billy to see it. The guys had brought plenty of good eats with them that had been prepared by John's grandmother. They headed towards San Patricio down a winded trail. After following the trail for a few miles they decided to stop and eat. After a few more miles of hiking, the trail started to get narrow and the wind began to pick up. They put scarves in front of their faces to block dust and sand from getting in heir eyes. Dustin thought he saw something around the corner. Then John started hearing things like horses coming down the trail so the boys hid behind some big boulders setting off the trail. John took off running down the trail toward Lincoln. Soon Dustin followed. Billy just stayed behind looking and waiting. Billy thought it was stupid of him to wait any longer so he took off to catch up with the others. The other boys were fast runners so it took Billy a while to get up with them. Finally they met up on a horse trail that took them down into Lincoln. It was getting late. They were all tired and hungry so they decided to go to the Wortley Hotel. Here, Glen prepared dinner for them.

Dustin, John and friend in Lincoln 1990

The Wortley Hotel where Billy Cox II a.k.a "The Kid" would stay

Afterwards, they all went back home. Billy's home was across the street from the hotel , next door to Raflita. The next day Billy helped Raflita carry her groceries inside her home. She always gave the kid a tip for helping her. Raflita was related to Sheriff Brady who was killed in 1878 in Lincoln.

Raflita who was related to Sheriff Brady

Kevin and Scott came to Lincoln to pick Billy up so that he could help them get water for the townspeople. In order to get drinking water they would have to go to the Baca Canyon where there was a natural spring. On their way, Deputy Mac told the boys to be careful because there were some cattle being taken nearby. He asked that if they saw any suspicious behavior to let him know. The boys agreed and continued on their way to get the water.

Scott and Kevin told Billy that people still rustled cattle in these days and times but it's done with trucks and tractor trailers. After bringing the water into town Billy, Kevin, Scott, Manny and Jack got ready to take a ride into White Oaks where there was a dance going on. There were pretty Spanish girls at the dance. Billy danced with a girl named Jennifer who was from Carrizozo, N.M. One week later Billy rode to the courthouse to meet up with Jack. Jack told Billy that Lincoln's annual fiesta was coming up this weekend. There would be people from all over this territory coming to the fiesta. All Billy could think about was all the pretty women that were sure to be there. The fiesta arrived an so did all of the Spanish people, Mexicans, Anglos, ranchers and bikers. The Mascarlaro Apachees came in from the surrounding hills for their Pow Wows. Jack, Manny and Scott were at the courthouse hanging out. Sheriff James rode in on his horse with his deputies by his side. James asked Billy what he thought of the New Mexican fiestas. Billy told him they were cool. The other deputies seemed to have other things on their minds, especially one deputy. It was Deputy Mac, also known as Mac. As the horse trotted by, Mac gave Billy a look to remember. Later Manny put his hand on Billy's shoulder and asked him if everything was alright. Billy told him that everything was fine. Billy wanted to go party. He was dancing with Barbara to a Garth Brooks song. There was a parade in town and Jack was driving the fire truck. Everyone wanted Billy to stand on top of the fire truck and lead the parade It was August of 1990 and it seemed as though Billy was settling in for an experience of his life. Some of the townspeople would give Billy their telephone numbers and ask him to look them up if he ever needed any food or a place to hang out. Billy kept this information to himself. During the fiesta Blake and Patrick started playing their guitars. They played hits from artists such as Paul McCartney and Van Morrison. Everyone danced to the music and was having a good time. Lacey and Dora who were the daughters of Joe joined in the music that Blake and Patrick were playing. They were terrific singers. Billy started thinking about some of his favorite hang outs. One in particular was the general store in Lincoln which was owned and managed by Darla and Harvey. Billy and his friends would visit the general store to buy most of the goods. Billy enjoyed the fresh coffee and homemade burritos that Darla would make. Later Billy ran into Jennifer whom he had met five months earlier in White Oaks. They took a walk down the trail that lead to the Rio Bonito River and talked about her future plans. She wanted to go to college in Texas but was not sure what to major in. Billy told her that she was young and that she should not worry to much about her future. "Everything happens for a reason", Billy said. Jennifer thought that if you did not have a proper education you would not amount to much in this world. "If you believe in the truth, you will know everything that you need to know and everything else means nothing", said Billy.

The trail that led to the Rio Bonito River

The Rio Bonito River in Lincoln, NM

Lincoln County Courthouse

This is where Ranger Jack and Billy would perform stories of Bonney's famous escape

Later that same day Billy headed back to the main street of Lincoln, where the fiesta was still going on. Jack and Manny came by, blazing on their four wheelers. Supposedly a fight broke out on the east end of town. Billy paid the situation no mind. He was getting hungry so he headed over to Darla's general store to buy a homemade burrito. He would then head down to the river trail over to the Ellis Store Bed and Breakfast. Billy's friends Blake, Patrick, Darush, Kevin and Manny were all at the B & B when he arrived. Blake yelled out Billy's name with enthusiasm. Everyone just looked around and sure enough a figure came up from the river. It was "The Kid". Blake told Billy a reporter was looking for him earlier, but they left for the west end of town.

A photo of early morning in Lincoln N.M.

Close friends of the Kids, Blake and Patrick at the Ellis Store

Bob, The Kid and friends at White Oaks Saloon

The fight that everyone assumed broke out earlier was not really a fight at all. Some of Blake's horses got out and had to be caught and returned to the corral. All of a sudden Billy and the boys heard music. It sounded like Indian style. It was the Apache's who had come in for their annual Pow Wows. Billy went over to the Pow Wow to watch the Indians dance. He even got the chance to meet Geronimo's great grandson which was a very neat experience. Billy later heads back to the general store to hang out with his friends and their family. As Billy was about to leave the store a stranger approached him. Billy backed up with caution. "You're him, aren't you?" asked the stranger. "What do you mean?" Billy asked. "Your William Cox II, Billy the Kid, said the man. I've come all the way from Phoenix, to take your picture. My name is Bob Boze Bell"

The Ranger Station in Lincoln, NM 1990

"Well, then let's get ready to take some pictures", Billy replied. Bob told Billy that he would take care of him financially. After the picture were taken Billy was immediately paid. He then caught a ride with Leroy to Roswell to deposit his money in the bank and later headed back to Lincoln. Billy and Kevin took a ride over to the Salazar canyon where Bob Boze Bell and his gang had set up their camp. Bob and his gang were riding over to the White Oaks Saloon to have a few drinks. Billy and Kevin were invited to go with them. After getting rowdy a bit they headed over to Carrizozo to Roy's General Store for a drink or two. Billy did not drink a lot so he just had a banana split with whip cream which he used in a toast.

Billy Cox II, The Kid, stayed here from time to time

DANCE

White Oaks Saloon

WHITE OAKS, NEW MEXICO

Sat., Nov. 23, 1991

9:00 PM to 1:00 AM

Featuring . . .

TERRY BULLARD & THE BULLETS

NO COVER CHARGE

After leaving Roy's General store Billy headed back to Salazar Canyon. Everyone was sitting around the fire telling stories and singing songs. It was getting close to dinner time so Bob threw some steaks and potatoes on the grill for everyone. After Billy and Kevin ate the food they thanked Bob for the food and told him that they needed to get back to Lincoln.

Roy at his General Store in Carrizozo, NM

The two boys headed back to the fiesta to find some senoritas. Billy ran into Robert who was leaving Lincoln and heading for Carrizozo. He told Billy that if he was in need of some work he could help him build a fence for his corral. Billy told Robert that he appreciated the offer and he would get back with him. It was around nine o'clock at night when Billy and Kevin got back to Lincoln. The fiesta was still going strong. Kevin and Billy headed over to Barbara's casa where there was a party going on. A lady walked up to Billy and said "So, you're the one I've been reading about". She then took Billy by the hand and led him out on the dance floor. They danced to Bad Company. They kissed and danced for hours.

Fort Stanton, NM 1990

102

Kevin had a girl who he was seeing at the time and Manny had his wife there. Billy invited the woman back to Jack's casa. Jack would be out for the night. She told Billy that she would go. As Billy was leaving he leaned over to Barbara to thank her for the party. She kissed him before he could finish his sentence. For a moment Billy thought maybe he should stay and see what would happen but instead decided to leave with the other lady since she seemed to be a sure thing.

Behind Manny's Casa in Lincoln, NM 1990

When they arrived at Jack's casa they continued to make out. The girl would not let Billy go any further. Before he knew it, the time was three o'clock in the morning. Billy was left on the couch with a sore mouth from kissing all night. He did not get any action that night. The girl decided to leave. Before she walked out the door she turned to Billy and said "You've got friends around here". Billy just looked at her with confusion and then drifted off to sleep. The next morning Billy slowly woke up. Kevin and Manny were just waking up as well. Manny's wife decided to make breakfast burritos for the guys. Billy stepped outside and saw people were packing up the fiesta and heading home. It was later August and September was slowly creeping up. Billy told his friends that the party was just getting started. Billy was in need of work. He headed over to Dr. Woods house to see if Jean knew anyone who was in need of a helper. She hooked him up with Buddy who was from El Capitan. Buddy built deer fences.

The Bluff behind Manny's casa in Lincoln, NM 1990

Buddy was in need of help in the Hondo Valley, on Mascalaro Apache Reservation or near it. He was to help build a deer fence approximately ten miles long. Billy had to share a tent with two Mexican men. There names were Paco and Francisco. The job site was out in the middle of nowhere. Billy had to use a rock bar for pounding through the rock. Working so hard in the intense New Mexico heat became old very quickly, but Billy still continued to work hard. In the middle of working one day Billy heard a gun shot. He ran toward the noise to see what had happened. Paco was holding up a dead rattle snake. He asked Billy if he liked snakes. "Hell no", Billy replied as he headed back to work. After a couple of weeks of hard work Billy's skin began to look very red and he was getting sick. He had been getting to much sun.

Five miles east of Lincoln, NM 1990

Buddy told Billy to rest in the tent and drink plenty of water. After a few days of rest Billy was feeling much better. This time Buddy put Billy on a different job. He had to paint the poles that Paco and Francisco had installed As he painted the poles Billy began to sing "Free Footin" which was an old song from the movie Tom Sawyer which Johnny Whitaker had sung. Buddy checked on Billy to see how the painting was coming along. Billy was just singing, painting and having a merry time. Suddenly four men came riding up on four wheelers. The men asked Buddy and Billy if they had seen any suspicious activity or any trucks in the area. The two replied no and asked what was wrong. They were told that some cattle were missing and truck tire tracks had been left behind. Buddy told the four men that if he did see anything he would be sure to radio them or the Sheriff. The men thanked Buddy and then drove away. Pounding the hard rock was getting harder and harder for the men in the increasing heat. Billy told Buddy that they made need to use dynamite on the areas where there was a lot of rock. Buddy informed Billy that this project was going to take at least one year to complete. Billy started shaking his head and wiping the sweat from his face. "I don't think I can handle a year of this", said Billy. Both of them began to laugh. Buddy told Billy that if he still needed extra money there were more odd jobs for him to take on. Billy was paid the money he was owed and Buddy gave him a ride back into Lincoln. He arrived there sometime in early September of 1990. He went to the Ellis Store to meet his friends Blake, Darush, Patrick, Manny and Scott for dinner. After dinner Buddy took plenty of groceries and beer back to Paco. Billy just took off his hat and kicked off his boots. Then he settled in for some relaxing music performed by Patrick and Blake. The next morning Billy threw his hat and boots back on as he headed over to the post office to check his mail. On his way there he was stopped by some people asking to take his picture. Billy took off his stove pipe hat and then held it out before him while saying "I'm open to small donations". The gentlemen wanting the picture placed a twenty dollar bill in the hat. Billy thanked the men, posed for the picture and then continued onward to the post office. The post master told Billy he had a lot of mail which had come in from all over the country.

Lincoln County Courthouse where William H. Bonney escaped in 1880

Billy took his mail and headed over to Jack's casa. On his way he looked up and saw Betty standing on her porch smoking a cigar. She gave Billy a look to remember.

This is where Betty and her family lived in Lincoln, NM

When Billy arrived at Jack's he was asked how the fence job was going. Billy smiled at Jack and then quickly changed the subject. Jack told Billy that Tom and Eric were in town to see him. They were staying at the Wortley Hotel. Billy decided to walk to the Wortley to pay them a visit. Tom and Eric had made plans to search for Coranados gold in the Capitan mountains and wanted Billy to join them. "Let's ride, boys", Billy eagerly responded. They had to go through Salazar and Baca canyons in order to go through Picacho canyon. They spent a few days in the mountains looking for the gold. Tom had acquired a map supposedly from the 1940's. He was told a man stumbled across some gold and tried to map out the area. Unfortunately no one ever saw the gold again nor could they remember the area in which it was found.

On the top of Capitan Peak there was a cabin for people to use incase they were caught in bad weather so the men decided to stay their nights in it. After no luck finding gold the men decided to head back down the mountains. The Kid was a little disappointed that they did not find any gold. While working their way through the mountains they came out at Arabela, which was just west of Hondo. Tom and Eric were heading back to Roswell so Billy asked them to drop him off at the post office in Hondo. He was dropped off just in time for the mail route coming in from Roswell and heading to Carrizozo which goes through the Lincoln route. Leroy was driving the mail truck that day so he gave Billy a ride and asked him how everything was going. Billy replied "I'm surviving". Leroy's ranch was always open to Billy. They were very good friends. Leroy took Billy back to Lincoln. Billy then walked over to Darla's house to see Dustin, Harvey and Kevin. Kevin told Billy that Deputy Mac wanted to see him. Billy replied "Oh yeah, what for?"

Eric, Tom and The Kid were looking for gold

Billy on top of Capitan Mountain and feeling on top of the world

Eric and Billy looking for gold, 1990

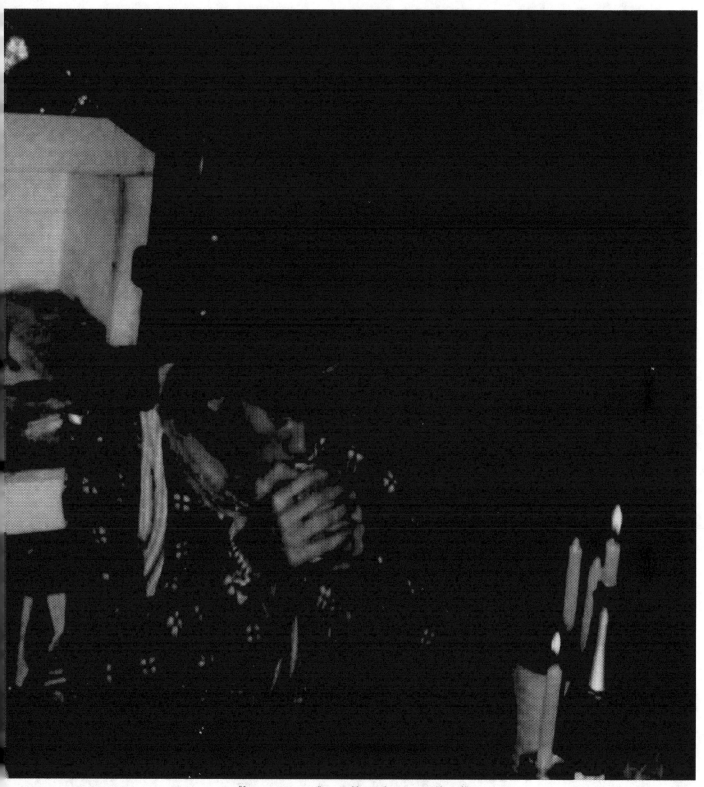

Billy warming himself with a cup of coffee

Above: The Capitan Gap in Lincoln county, 1990

The Capitan Peak, 1990

Leroy and good friend in Carrizozo, NM 1990

Kevin told Billy that he was not sure. He thought maybe it had something to do with old Bob on the east side of town. Billy walked outside to get some fresh air and noticed that there was a storm heading in. The wind was really picking up and blowing leaves around on the street. He looked to the west and standing near Tunstall's store was Deputy Mac. "Can I have a word with you?" asked Mac. "Sure", answered Billy. Mac wanted to know about the volunteer job that Bob at the trust had offered him.

Bob in Lincoln, NM

Billy told Mac that he was fine with Jack and with the state. "Is that so?", said Mac. Mac then told him that some of the ranchers thought Billy and his friends were responsible for the recent cattle theft. "What"! Billy shouted. Again, Mac reminded Billy not to think to long about it and then he sped off in his Blazer. Before leaving Mac gave Billy his card and asked that he call when he was ready to talk or as he had put it "When Lincoln gets too cold". Billy could not believe what had just happened.

He was being accused of shooting and stealing cattle. Manny and Joe approached Billy about the news. By now the rumor was all over Lincoln. Manny and Joe told Billy what was happening to him was simply bull and that he shouldn't go down without a fight. Jack had left for Santa Fe to meet with the state officials about money coming into Lincoln. He wanted to find new ways to bring in the revenue. He also brought forward another concern. Semi trucks had been racing down the street through Lincoln causing the buildings to shake. Over time this could cause a lot of trouble for the structures. Manny, Joe and Billy paid a visit to Blake, Patrick and the boys at the Ellis Store. Blake was outside feeding his horses. Billy told Blake about the news which he had already known about. He told Billy not to sweat it and that people in the town had forgot what it was like to be young. It was now October and Billy was staying at the Ellis Store helping out with the fence work, feeding the cattle and horses and cleaning up after the animals. Sometimes the smell was so unbearable that it almost knocked Billy over. Billy caught a ride with Robert who also drove the mail truck. He was heading to Roswell. Once he got there he deposited some more money into his bank account. Then he was off to Ken and Donna's house for dinner. Billy told the family about the rumors circulating around Lincoln. Ken just dropped his fork down onto his plate with a look of disbelief. He told Billy to stay away from Lincoln. He believed that the townspeople were trying to start the problems up again after all these years. "Stay in Roswell, Billy", said Ken. "I have done nothing wrong, said Billy. I have brought peace to that town and I will be damned if I am going to allow those sons of bitches to run me out! Old Bobby boy thinks he's running this game but, he's unaware of whose really running this show". Billy just sat back and smiled. After a few days at Ken and Donna's home Billy left for Tom's ranch taking a short cut. Donna had packed him some burritos for his trip. Billy was letting Tom and Don, who was a biker from the old school, know about the rumors in Lincoln. Don just started laughing. He then told Billy that he could arrange for some other bikers from the area to ride through Lincoln sending the people a message. To ease Billy's tension Don suggested that the three of them go to the dance in White Oaks that was happening that night.

Tom, Don and Billy in Roswell, NM 1990

115

The Kid's friend Scott riding the old trails of Lincoln

Billy made plans to take another route from Roswell to Capitan to get to White Oaks. Tom assured Billy that everything was going to be alright. Little Bobby, his brother Billy, Sammy and Eddie were outside playing and having a good time. The Kid decided to join them in the fun. After a few days of staying at Tom's house Billy headed back to the post office to catch a ride with the mail carrier to Lincoln. Billy was telling Leroy about the dance that he, Tom and Don had attended in White Oaks. Leroy too told Billy that he should not worry about the trouble in Lincoln. Leroy had also been staying busy with his work at his ranch in Carrizozo. An hour later Billy was dropped off at the Ellis Store.

Blake, Scott and Patrick were working at the ranch as usual. The boys looked down as Billy walked up to them. Blake informed Billy that Mac had come around again and was threatening to take Billy and the boys in if he could catch them. He also told Billy that he knew he was innocent but that some of the townspeople had a problem with him. Kevin came over to visit with everyone. He asked Billy if he wanted to make ten dollars an hour helping his stepfather Ron build a shed down the street. Billy accepted the offer. Kevin, Ron and Billy got together for breakfast at the Wortley Hotel. Sam, who was a rancher in the Baca Canyon area, was also having breakfast at the hotel with some other ranchers. Billy did not like Sam because he thought he was a drunk that talked to much. "Hey Kid, have you been messing around on my ranch?" Sam yelled over to Billy. Kevin and Ron stood up from their chairs and took up for Billy. Ron told Sam that Billy worked for him and didn't have to mess with anyone's ranch. Kevin then said that harassment was against the law. "Not in Lincoln county", said Sam. He and the other ranchers started laughing.

Bob the traveling artist standing in front of the Lincoln County Courthouse

As Billy and his friends finished their meal and headed out the door Billy turned to Sam and said "I hear you like to drink a lot". "I damn sure do boy, what's it to you?" asked Sam. The Kid replied "I don't think you drink enough, Sam". Billy just smiled and then continued out the door and headed to work. After work Billy met two fellows from Arizona. Their names were Billy C and Gary. They were staying at the Wortley Hotel. Billy C was a writer who was often seen with his pipe in his mouth. He was thinking of moving to Carrizozo. Gary and Billy C told the kid that they had read about him in Tuscan, A.Z. The Kid asked them if what they had read was good or bad. "All good", they replied. The two men told Billy that if he was ever to visit Carrizozo he could stay with them for a while. Billy appreciated the offer. Later the Kid headed back over to the Ellis Store where he saw Blake, Patrick and Jack. Billy and Jack took a ride to get some groceries. They spotted Scott near a plaza painting. He told Jack that he could use Billy's help next week. Billy agreed to help. So, the next week he began helping Scott paint a building in Ruidosa. Scott was a good guy.

In the distance Capitan Mountains, 1990

He was always hooking Billy up with odd jobs to put a little money in the Kid's pocket. Scott also lived in Lincoln and would pick Billy up at the Ellis Store for work. Billy C and Gary decided to settle in Carrizozo. They looked Billy up in Lincoln because they were going to Glencoe to find Tunstall's murder site and also to camp out for a few days. Since Billy's job with Scott had just ended he was free to join them. As they headed off for the journey they soon discovered it would not be easy. It took hours tying to find the old trail. Once they got close they had to follow red arrows pointing about one hundred yards off the trail where Tunstall and his horse were shot. Once they arrived at the site they saw a large rock with a plaque that read Tunstall's murder site. These words sent a chill up the kid's spine.

Billy Cox II, The Kid, asleep in a tree at John Tunstall's murder site

Gary and Billy C asked Billy if he was feeling alright. Billy looked at his friends and asked "How could someone just shoot a man down like a dog? I guess it was for the same reason someone blew a hole through JFK's head; it was for money". The kid just looked back at the rock with disbelief. "Well, I guess it doesn't matter now", said Billy. "Why?" asked his friends. "Because they all are dead now and I believe they got their punishment", said Billy laughing quietly.

At the end of the trail lie McSwain and Tunstall's graves

Billy C and Gary asked the kid if he was ready to go find a place to set up camp. They headed east three miles down a dirt road. They set up camp behind a hill down an old trail. Gary and the kid built a fire and threw some nice looking steaks on the coals. They also wrapped up some potatoes in foil and cooked them on the fire. The kid told Billy C and Gary that he figured they heard of his troubles in Lincoln. As Gary chewed his steak he nodded his head up and down. He told Billy not to sweat the heat he was getting and asked him never to back down. He told Billy that people were starting the rumors because he was getting a lot of publicity. "You're a free-lance, Billy, said Gary. Some folks don't like when you try to do something unique". "All I want to do is be free and bring people together in unity because one day we will all pass and the resentment and hate won't matter anymore", replied the kid. "That's the truth but, sometimes people won't care about the truth until they are on their last breath", said Gary. The kid's friends reminded him to keep his true friends close to him, especially while making his way through this uncanny experience. Billy raised to his feet and looked at his friends. "Are you guys my true friends?" he asked. "Yes, we are", said Gary and Billy C. The kid just smiled and asked them to put on some of their Irish music they had brought along. They spent a good part of the night eating, talking about history and listening to good music. Later as Billy laid in his sleeping bag he looked up at the stars and asked God to guide him in the right direction. Then he watched the fire slowly burn down as he drifted off to sleep. The next morning the kid got up and went for a hike in the hills by himself. As Billy headed around a hill he saw sticks that were neatly tied together with yellow, red and white ribbons. He stood still for a moment and realized that the wind was slowly blowing in that one area. He looked around and saw that the leaves on the other trees were completely still. He got scared and grabbed his knife. Billy did not know what to make of this. The kid thought it might be an Indian spirit grave site. He slowly started walking backwards and then turned to run back to camp where he told his friends what had happened. They too thought it was strange. After a few days the men decided to head back to Lincoln.

Manny on his ranch just three miles east of Lincoln

The kid told his friends about the old Ft. Stanton trail in Glencoe that went through Devil's Canyon that lead to Lincoln. Manny had taken the kid on the trail several times so he knew it very well. So, they decided to take that route, which was a rocky one. Finally Billy C and Gary brought the kid back to the Ellis Store and then headed home themselves. It was starting to get very cold as November was fast approaching. Billy enjoyed the cold weather in New Mexico. It was really nice, especially at night time. Air conditioning was not necessary. He could just open a window and enjoy the cool night breeze. Billy would tell his friends that he could feel the magic in the air. He decided to ask Blake, Patrick and the other boys what the latest gossip in Lincoln was. They told Billy that after everything had hit the ceiling it began to die down. Later, Billy walked over to Sharon's house for dinner. Kevin, Jack and Manny were all joined at the dinner table too. During the meal Billy asked Jack who he thought could be behind the accusations. Jack said he thought it could be coming from the west side of town. Manny warned Billy to watch out for Sam.

Ranger Manny who was a good friend of Billy Cox II

Billy knew Sam was a problem but had not considered him enough of a threat to be worried about him. Some thought it could have been old Betty and her bunch of rowdy cowboys. One thing was certain. A large group of people had to be involved for deputy Mac to come around harassing folks. Jack said that there were people in Lincoln that wanted the kid to stay and some that wanted him ran out. "Damn, I wish they would make up their minds, said the kid. Do they want me to stay or go?" Everyone at the table including the kid started laughing and then finished their dinner. Sharon surprised her guests with a homemade cherry pie. The men were grateful. Afterwards, Manny and Billy cut out a little early and headed to Manny's ranch. He let Billy know that he would always have the support of his family. Billy appreciated that. Manny's wife Silvia showed Billy to the guest room where he spent the night. About two weeks later a friend of the kid's named Eddie came by from Roswell to go hunting in Nogal Canyon. He invited Billy to go with him. The two of them headed off to the canyon in hopes of catching a couple of bucks.

The kid hunting in Nogal Canyon

As they hid in the bushes, so did the deer. "The deer must know when it's hunting season, said Billy. I think they're as smart as we are". They stayed in Eddie's cabin for two days. There was about five inches of snow on the ground and no deer to hunt. Billy told Eddie if he really wanted some deer he knew where they could get some. So after a couple of days they headed back to Lincoln and over to Manny's ranch. Manny took them into his big freezer. The kid opened the door and said "There's your deer and a freezer full of it too". Manny told Eddie that hunters spook deer out of the bigger mountains and the deer run into the foothills which follow the Rio Bonito that ends up on his land. Then I just sit and wait with my thirty-thirty Winchester. Manny and Billy told Eddie to take as much deer meat as he wanted. Eddie thanked them, piled some deer meat into his cooler and headed back to Roswell. The kid shook Manny's hand and thanked him for hooking Eddie up. "What are friends for", said Manny. "We are definitely true friends to the end", said Billy. Later Manny and the kid headed over to the Ellis Store to hang with the boys. Darush was working on a CD and had got signed in Europe. Blake and Patrick had capitalized their own CD out called "My brother and his friend". Billy especially loved their song "As long as we're together". Thanksgiving was now just a few days away. Patrick, Blake and Darush got a large turkey and cooked it behind the mill house. It was a beautiful Thanksgiving day. Billy had a lot of friends and their families around him. It was a quiet day in Lincoln. Before everyone knew it December had rolled in. It was getting colder and colder. When it snowed the main street of the town looked like a white sheet. Whether it was the year 1880 or 1990 Lincoln looked the same. Everyone was staying quite busy. Jack had to go to Santa Fe for business while Bob from the trust went to Mesilla to a historical meeting.

Billy and Bob in Lincoln, NM 1990

Kevin's step-father was doing some work at the horse museum in Ruidoso and wanted Billy and Kevin to help him with some odd jobs there. On December the thirteenth Billy celebrated his birthday at Kevin's house. Darla brought a big chocolate cake which was Billy's favorite. Later the guys all played down at the river. Dustin had a small boat which he brought down to the river for everyone to take turns riding in it. Weeks later Christmas arrived and Darla had invited Billy to a church celebration at the base of the Capitan Mountains. Everyone brought a gift to exchange. People brought Billy jewelry like necklaces and bracelets. He was also given candy. After the function ended Billy thanked everyone for the gifts and in turn they thanked him for the gift he had given them. Everyone was now getting ready to celebrate New Year's Eve in Lincoln. Billy was getting excited about the New Year's Eve party at Barbara's house. It was December thirty first and cowboys, cowgirls, bikers and lawmen headed into Lincoln to ring in the new year. There were a lot of parties going on all throughout the county but Billy decided to spend his celebration at Barbara's house with the gang. The kid had a lot of supporters there. It was indeed a very wild party. There was a lot of drinking going on and people were getting high. Women started stripping off their clothes. When midnight arrived a lot of the men started shooting their guns in the air while everyone was yelling "Happy New Year!" A lot of people were singing Auld Lang Syne. There were camp outs going on all over the town, but Billy and some of his friends decided to sleep at the park next to the Rio Bonito. It was very cold but Billy's sleeping bag and clothes kept him warm. The next morning Billy went over to Darla's casa to take a bath and grab some lunch. Billy asked Kevin how he ended up on the bench at the park. Kevin told Billy that it was because he had a few too many drinks in him. Everyone started laughing. Things were pretty quite in Lincoln. Billy was spending most of his time doing odd jobs up and down Lincoln. Billy paid a visit to Leroy in Carrizozo. It just so happened that Leroy needed a hand building a fence at his ranch. He had a bunk house out back where Billy could stay for a few weeks. Carrizozo was just outside of the mountains and was located in the desert. A winter storm was coming in and brought strong winds. Billy would stare out the window and watch as tumbleweeds would blow by. It started to snow and the bunk house would shake all throughout the night because of the strong winds. The kid threw on his scarf and hat so that he could take a walk outside. He loved the energy he felt from the storm. Billy walked away from the ranch and out to the desert. Snow flurries were all around him. Billy went to see Leroy's horse. He approached him with caution and then slowly began petting him. The kid had always wondered what it would be like to jump on a horse and just take off. Not since his childhood days had Billy rode on a horse. He still remembered the basics and figured that if he pulled the reigns left, right and back the horse was sure to obey him. However, the horse could sense Billy's fear and ignored the commands.

A few miles west of Lincoln which was near Scott's ranch

Five miles east of Lincoln, NM

Instead he wildly galloped off into the desert. The kid desperately tried to stop the horse. The animal seemed out of control and did not allow Billy to regain control. At this point he got very scared that the horse would throw him off. All of the sudden the horse made a u-turn and hauled ass back to the ranch. Billy held on tightly until the horse reached Leroy's back door. Leroy heard the noise and opened the door. The sight of the frazzled kid made him laugh. Billy asked "What's so funny?" "You are", said Leroy. Billy told Leroy all he was trying to do was take the horse for a ride. "Oh, I think the horse took you for a ride instead", said Leroy. Come to find out, Leroy had been watching Billy from the window and had been cracking up at him the entire time. "I guess I will just have to learn to ride better", said Billy. Leroy warned Billy that if he allowed the horse to smell his fear he would never be able to control him. Leroy walked the horse back to the corral while Billy grabbed a bail of hay and threw it to the horse. The horse started eating right away. "Hell, I guess that's what he really wanted", said Billy. After a few days of working on the ranch Billy and Leroy went over to the White Oaks Saloon to knock back a couple of drafts. Leroy asked Billy if he had ever taken the back way from White Oaks to El Capitan. Billy replied yes. He and Blake had taken the trail before coming from Lincoln. Leroy and Billy headed over to Capitan for supplies. On the way there Leroy began talking about his days in Vietnam. He told Billy each day when he woke up he wondered if today would be his last. Billy just put his head down in respect. Leroy told Billy that he read his story of how he lost his mother to suicide at the age of thirteen. He told Billy that it is a very heavy thing to loose your mother at such a young age especially with such a dramatic death. "You've really been there man", said Leroy. "Yeah, but it doesn't matter now, said Billy. It happened such a long time ago". Soon they arrived at the saw shop in El Capitan where Harvey and Joe worked. Leroy picked up a saw and some wood and then headed over to Spanky's to eat. Jack and Manny were eating there too. After Billy and Leroy visited with their friends for a while they headed back to White Oaks and then to Carrizozo. They saw that Robert was building a fence so they decided to stop and help him out as well as shoot the breeze while they were there.

Robert and his gang building a fence in Carrizozo, NM

Robert in Carrizozo, NM 1990

Robert raised a lot of chickens and a few cattle. This kept him very busy when he wasn't driving the mail route. After a couple of days of working they headed over to Roy's General Store to visit and have some ice cream. "Business is good", Roy said to them. Roy asked Billy if he had been in Lincoln lately. Billy told him that he had been at Leroy's ranch working for the past several days. When Billy went to Lincoln it was usually at night time so that Deputy Mac wouldn't harass him.

However, the rumors were all dying down so it was getting pretty quite. Gary and Billy C had been at Roy's asking when the kid was going to visit again. After their visit Billy went back to the ranch. He told Leroy that he might go and hang out with Gary and Billy C for a few days while the kid was in Carrizozo. Leroy told Billy to take some deer meat from the freezer and bring it to his friends. So he did and started heading to Carrizozo. It was now early February 1991. When they pulled up to his friend's casa he saw Billy C sitting on the porch smoking a pipe and writing. "So, how have you been kid?" asked Billy C. "I've been mighty fine, said the kid. I have been keeping busy working over at Leroy's ranch trying to earn a little extra cash". The kid told him that he was thinking of visiting for a few days and asked if that would be alright. Billy C told the kid that was fine and said that his room was in back where he had left it. The kid gave the deer meat he had brought to Gary so that he could freeze it. Gary asked the kid if he knew Jim P who owns and operates the saloon in White Oaks. The kid told Gary that he had met Jim a couple of times but did not know him personally. Gary told the kid that he was working on drumming up some business opportunities and may have a space for him. The kid asked Billy C and Gary if they wanted to go to White Oaks and hang out and then possibly head to the Corona area to see what's happening there. There was a saloon in Corona that Gary was fond of so they all stopped in and had a couple of drinks. Gary liked his rum and Cokes. Billy started talking to an older biker chic who even gave him her phone number for future reference. Billy slowed danced with her for a while and then it was time to head on. They all went over to a friend of Gary's who owned a ranch and an antique store between White Oaks and Corona. This was also near an old place where a group of young outlaws used to hang out over one hundred and twenty-five years ago. The place where they used to hang was called the Great House Ranch and Saloon which is no longer standing. Gary's friend was a nice old lady who had lived in that area of New Mexico for over fifty years. Gary introduced his friend to young Billy. The kid enjoyed looking around her store. The lady told the kid that she had read a lot about him and asked if he had returned to haunt everyone. "Not to haunt anyone, just to love everyone", the kid replied. The lady told Billy that she hoped he would love the beautiful dinner that she had prepared for he and his friends. After dinner the kid and his friends thanked her for the wonderful meal and left the village near Ancho and then headed back to White Oaks where Billy was formally introduced to Jim, the owner. Jim's brothers were in the cherry business back east in Michigan. They also owned a Christmas tree lot in Tucson, Arizona. During Christmas time Jim would help his brother Walter sell Christmas trees. He thought he might be able to use Gary's business experience in the future. Jim bought Gary a couple of drinks while Billy sipped on a Coke. Billy C just sat there smoking his pipe. As it got later the men decided to head down an old winded road that took them towards highway 54 and over to Carrizozo. Days later the kid, Gary and Billy C went to Roswell so Billy could once again drop some money in the bank. Later it was over to Ken and Donna's house for a visit. Ken told Billy that Tom and Don are on the Pecos River hunting wild hogs. Billy hoped that Tom would catch a hog. He knew Tom was a very good shot. After visiting with Ken for a few hours they decided to head back to Lincoln county, Carrizozo. They took the old Pine Ridge Road which was the old trail that came out in Capitan. Then they took 380 west to Carrizozo. Things were going very well for Billy. He had money in the bank as well as being free as a bird and doing whatever he liked. Gary brought Billy another news article written about him.

The kid just laughed. A couple of weeks later Billy decided to head over to Roswell to see how Tom's hunting trip had gone. Tom had indeed caught himself a fine hog. Don had run out of bullets after a couple of days so Tom just loaned him his rifle and then headed back to his casa. Soon Don caught a hog and then cut it up and put it in his freezer. He then headed over to Tom's to drop off his rifle. Tom told Billy that he came to Roswell just in time. Tom had to take a trip to California to see his brother for a couple of weeks and wondered if Billy would stay and watch his house for him. Billy told Tom that he would be happy to stay. He told Billy that there was plenty of deer and hog meat as well as rabbit stew for him to eat. There was also a large stack of wood because it could get very cold. He also asked Billy to feed his dog Cocoa. Billy was shown where Tom's rifle was kept in case of an emergency. Pointing the rifle away from Billy, Tom switched the safety off and let his finger barely touch the trigger. All of the sudden the gun went off making a loud boom! Tom and Billy were both starring at each other in shock. Tom asked Billy if he was alright. He told Tom that he had soiled his pants and needed to use the bathroom. Tom apologized to Billy for what had happened and said that Don had a habit of leaving his rifle loaded when returning it. He also said that this would be the last time Don would be allowed to borrow it. A few days later Tom packs up and gets ready for his trip to California. It was March and still getting cold outside. It would still snow once in a while. Billy held down the fort for two weeks while Tom was away. He spent a lot of time splitting and stacking fire wood so he could use it at night to stay warm. Sammy, Eddie, Bobby and his brother Billy Jr would come over to play baseball. The kid would go over to Bobby and Billy Jr's parents house for dinner sometimes. Eddie and Sammy would often join them. Shannon and Tim came over to Tom's house to ask Billy if he wanted to go with them to the bottomless lake state park to go hiking. After hiking for a while Tim and Shannon found some Indian drawings on some rocks. They showed them to Billy. They decided to put some small rocks in a canyon and use them for target shooting Shannon could hit every rock. He was a great shot. After hanging in the desert for a while they got hungry and decided to cook up some deer meat Billy had brought from Tom's house. Later they all headed back to Roswell. After a couple of weeks Tom came back from his trip. Billy told Tom it was nice to have him back. "Good to see you too", Tom told Billy. They sat down and had a long talk about Tom's trip. Billy told Tom they should make an appearance in Lincoln. "Let's ride", said Tom. Billy and Tom arrived in Lincoln sometime in April of 1991. It was still very cold, especially at night time. The days were starting to get a little warmer. Tom and Billy headed straight over to the Ellis store to visit with Patrick and Blake and asked them if there was any work. Blake told Billy that the roof on the Ellis Store had not been re-done since the 1960's and they were about to put on a new one. There were wooden shingles on the roof. Scott was heading up the job and said that he could use Billy's help. Tom told the kid he had to go to Hondo to see a friend about some business and would check back with him in a few days. Billy was glad to get back to work. He started singing the song "Free Footin". "Are you singing that damn song again?" asked Scott. Billy just laughed and kept on singing and working. Scott went back inside the store to get more nails while Billy took a break. A blue pickup truck stopped on the main road in front of the Ellis Store about fifty yards from the kid. A man got out of the truck and stared at Billy while twirling a pistol and laughing.

Billy looked back at the man with concern. Then the stranger just got back in his truck and sped away. Patrick and Scott came walking around the corner with some supplies. Billy told them what had just happened and this caused them all to be concerned. The kid viewed this as a threat. Suddenly a Bronco came pulling up. It was deputy Mac. He stepped out of his vehicle and asked to speak with Billy. The kid asked Mac if he had driven all this way just to say hello. Blake, Scott and Patrick stood close to Billy's side. Blake told Mac that Billy had been staying and working with them. Mac told Blake that was real good. "I'm glad to see that you guys are taking such good care of our Billy", said Mac. As Mac was getting back into his Bronco Billy took out a business card the deputy had given to him a while ago. On the back of the business card was written the name of a well known lawyer. "Hey deputy, do you have another business card?" asked Billy. "Sure", said Mac. Then he bent down to give the card to Billy. The kid's wallet was open with the old card showing the lawyer's number. He wanted to make sure that Mac saw it. Billy hoped that this bluff would make Mac think twice before harassing him again. The kid went to see Jack about the problem. Jack told him that he was going to take a trip to see the state officials about this issue. The state supported Billy because of the money he was bring-ing in. Jack was going to speak with the sheriff of Lincoln county, James, about who was caus-ing this trouble. The one thing Billy did not want to see happen did happen. The trouble hit the news and now everyone knew about it. Billy knew that it was Bob at the east end of town. It was about people who wanted to control Billy and could not do it. There were people coming out of the woodwork that were saying they did believe that Billy had stolen and shot cattle. Billy read lies in the local paper about him breaking into the Wortley Hotel and sleeping in room number five. Billy looked at the boys and said "Hell, I've only stayed at the Wortley a couple of times in room number five and I was invited if you know what I mean and boy were they fine". Blake and the boys looked at Billy as if he was crazy. Patrick told Billy that no one cares about the women he stayed with at the Wortley. He was in trouble here. Billy didn't know what to do yet but he had a plan. Jack had a talk with Mac and so did other friends of Billy's. Billy went to Carrizozo to talk with Leroy about the situation in Lincoln. Leroy told Billy that he read about the trouble in the papers and he knew it was all made up. Leroy told Billy that when the truth crumbles to the earth it always rises again. He told Billy not to worry and asked him to go with him to get something to eat. After a couple of days in Carrizozo Billy rode over to San Patricio to visit a friend who he had met through Manny. Here he could lay low for a few days. Billy would hang out and walk to the apple orchard to help pick apples. Billy didn't want to be in Lincoln because of the trouble. Billy's friends told him that the news in Lincoln was that Mac was looking for him. A few days later Billy headed to Hondo to see friends and he was nervous not knowing what to do. Billy waited by the post office in Hondo for the mail route in which Leroy would be driving that day. Leroy took Billy through Lincoln on the way to Carri-zozo. Carrizozo was the county seat and that was were James was when Billy went to see him for some last support. "I guess they plan on running me out of town without a fight, said Billy. I'm innocent and no one has come to my aid". James told Billy that he was a good person and unfortunately there are a lot of jealous people out there. He told Billy to be aware of this. Billy needed to have a plan. James shook the kid's hand and wished him luck. Later the kid headed over to Billy C and Gary's casa. Gary and Billy C were in Lincoln today and things were stirred up there. Billy C told the kid that a lady named Bonnie was asking about him in town. Bonnie was from Alburg and was a writer. She was also good friends with Jack.

Billy was really afraid of what might happen to him and what lengths certain people would go to in order to run him out of town. However, he did have a plan. He would wait for the right time to make it happen. Billy needed to talk to Jack but, Jack was in Lincoln which is not where Billy wanted to be. He would need to go into town at night time so that no one could spot him. When the sun went down Billy crept into Lincoln and had a talk with Jack about the trouble. Billy told Jack that people were trying to interrupt his experience with their lies and conspiracy. Jack did agree with Billy but told him that this is reality and asked the kid what he planned on doing about it. Jack asked Billy if he had plans to go back to the east coast. Billy replied "I will not be going to the east coast but instead the northeast". The kid just smiled at Jack. Jack asked Billy what he meant by the northeast. "Soon, Jack, you will know what I mean and so will those bastards that are trying to run me out", said Billy. Jack asked Billy where he was going. Billy told Jack that he would let him know in time. He then said good night and left. He decided not to stay in Lincoln that night so he went back to Billy C and Gary's place. Billy stayed in Carri-zozo for a few weeks just buying time. Bonnie found Billy and met with him at Roy's General Store. She brought a friend of hers from Santa Fe. His name was Richard who was a syndicated writer and wanted to interview the kid. The article would be about Billy's side of the story. They talked about how nothing like this had ever happened to anyone and would probably never happen again as the story unfolds. They talked about his trouble and being unjustly ac-cused of a crime everybody knew he really did not do. Towards the end of the story Richard asked Billy what his future plans were. Billy told Richard that Lincoln was to hot for him right now and that he might go to Ft. Sumner for a while to cool down. Everyone started laughing. Billy stood up looking into the big mirror behind the bar and told everybody "We're going to have some fun now in Lincoln. He then said goodbye to everyone and bolted out the door and over to Leroy's for dinner. After a few days at Leroy's ranch Billy crept over to the Ellis Store in Lincoln were the boys were. Blake told Billy that he shouldn't take such a big risk coming there. He said that someone will find out that he's in Lincoln. "I just want to stay a couple of days", the kid told Blake. Blake told Billy that he was more than welcome to stay for a couple of days and that he could stay in the old mill house in the back. Times seemed to be changing at the Ellis Store. Blake told Billy that Darush is going back to Midland, TX to push his music and Patrick is going to be in Ruidoso for the next couple of days rehearsing with his band. Blake was going to head to Santa Fe to visit his parents for a couple of weeks. So, basically Billy was going to be there by himself at the Ellis Store. The mill house where Billy would sleep was used as nursing quarters in the 1800's. A lot of people died of tuberculosis in the mill house. On the second night that Billy was there it was nearing June 1, 1991, which would soon be one of the scariest nights of his life. A bad storm was coming in. There was a lot of wind and the shutters were banging fiercely against the windows. He could hear loud thunder and the room would light up from the intense lightning. It sounded like footsteps coming up the narrow steps to the second floor where he was staying. Billy slept with one eye open the entire night. The doors to some of the rooms were opening and closing. Billy grabbed his gun, not sure what to do. After a few hours of listening to all of the noises, Billy decided it wasn't worth it to stay there so he headed over to a friend's house who was leaving early in the morning for Ft. Sumner.

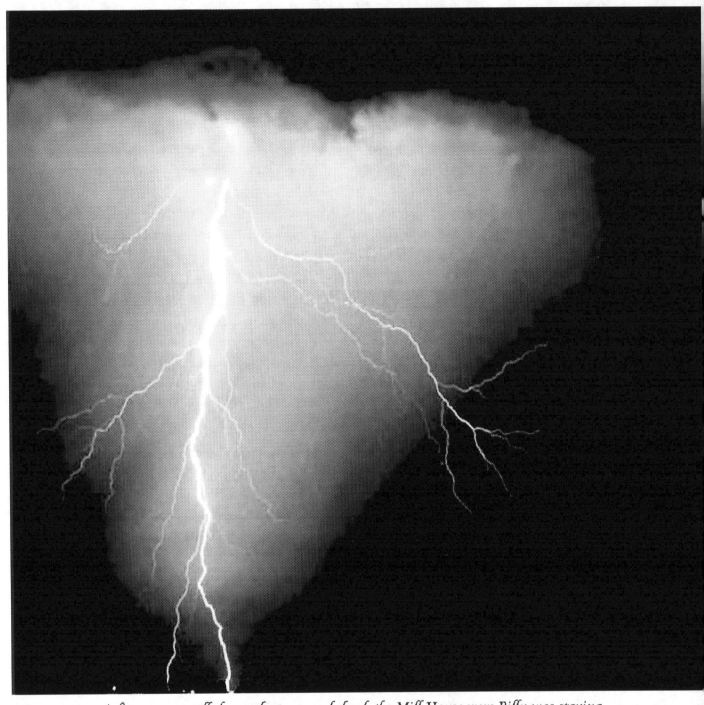

A fierce storm rolled over the town and shook the Mill House were Billy was staying

Jennifer, who was a good friend of Billy's

Billy's friend Crystal who was a close friend and was from the Mesilla/Los Crusas area

When the sun came up, Billy and his friend were bound for Ft. Sumner. Ft. Sumner was about one hundred and twenty miles northeast of Lincoln. When Billy arrived in town the people welcomed him with open arms. The story that Richard had written came out around the state of New Mexico that day of June 3, 1991. While the kid was in Ft. Sumner, Lincoln got a slap in the face. While in town Billy and his friend rode to Taiban to see Joe and let him know that the kid was in the area. Joe knew Billy had some problems in Lincoln but he told Billy that everybody had problems with that town. Even Lincoln took Ft. Sumner to court during the 1960's over the remains of William H. Bonney. So, that's why Ft. Sumner was so welcoming to the kid. Billy's friend left for Santa Rosa while Billy stayed behind. Joe told Billy he could help at the Big Indian Store for a few days. Joe had an extra room in the back. The store was the only building around for miles. Marilyn, who was Joe's wife, was a very nice lady. She would often cook meals for Billy. The kid met Derrell, who worked behind the counter and register of the store. Derrell and Billy became good friends and would often hang out.

Derrell and Billy taking a break in Taiban, NM

136

Lincoln visitors say they've seen a ghost

by Richard McCord Sumners Syndicate

In the summer of 1989, 22-year-old Billy Cox of Bartow, Florida, got a hankering to go west for the first time, looking for adventure.

He got off the Greyhound bus in Roswell and wandered into the local museum. The historian there, Ken Hobbs, took one look at him, gasped, and pronounced him a dead ringer for the most famous outlaw ever to wander through those parts: Billy the Kid.

For Cox, it was the start of something ... well, peculiar.

A few days later Hobbs drove Billy Cox to the town of Lincoln, where the Kid killed several men before he was gunned down at Fort Sumner in 1881 by Sheriff Pat Garrett, at the age of 21.

These events are now memorialized in a state monument, run by Ranger Jack Rigney. "This is Billy the Kid from Florida," Hobbs said to his friend the ranger — and Rigney could not believe his eyes.

Only one authenticated photograph of the Kid is known to exist. In it he wears a crumpled top hat, a low-slung gunbelt and a bandanna, and holds a Winchester rifle by his side. The camera captures his face straight-on. The face is identical to Billy Cox's.

When the ranger caught his breath, he and Cox struck a quick rapport. They stayed in touch after Billy took the bus back home and resumed his work as a busboy in a restaurant. Rigney visited relatives in Florida that winter and stopped by to see Billy, who had rounded up some clothes such as the Kid wore in the old tintype photo, and had been practicing the same pose.

As soon as Rigney saw Billy Cox intentionally impersonating Billy the Kid, he began seeing possibilities. So he suggested that Cox spend the next summer in Lincoln, to see what would happen.

"Jack even said there could be a 'financial supplement' to this," Billy remembers. "But I wasn't so sure what he meant."

Billy returned to Lincoln in July 1990, and stayed in a room in Rigney's house. As he walked through town, packing an unloaded pistol and a Winchester, tourists pointed at him in astonishment.

Then they wanted him to pose for photographs and paid him five or ten dollars without him having to ask. When there was a crowd, he could pick up $30 or $40 at a time.

At daily presentations at the state monument, Rigney would tell the story of Billy the Kid, then ask if anyone believed in ghosts. On cue, Cox would walk in and strike the pose. The tourists would gasp, grab for their cameras — and leave a donation.

In his spare time, Cox tried to do things that the first Billy had done in Lincoln County, more than 100 years ago. He borrowed horses and went riding through open country. He slept out under the stars. He did odd jobs on area ranches. He stopped to chat with everybody in town, and accepted handouts at many houses. He went to saloons in the old village of White Oaks, where señoritas would dance with him and call him "Billito."

Yet Cox insists he retained his own identity. He never felt he was mystically bonded with the Kid, much less a reincarnation.

"I was always William H. Cox, not William H. Bonney," he says.

"There were never any spirits in the night."

In this fashion, the summer passed. Capitalizing on New Mexico's unending fascination with its most notorious son, Cox portrayed Billy not only in Lincoln but also at festivals in Truth or Consequences and Taiban, and at the Eastern State Fair in Roswell. He won look-alike contests, staged shootouts with "Pat Garrett's Gang," was featured on local television and in national magazines, even had a videotape made about him. The pay was always chancy, but enough to keep him in canned pork and beans.

But the tourist season finally ended — and last October Cox realized things were changing. Rigney, in whose house he had lived all summer, started dropping hints about Florida. Then the deputy sheriff in Lincoln drove up one day and asked him outright: "when you going back home, Billy?"

Some cattle on nearby ranches had been shot, it seemed, and people suspected him. "The deputy thought I was getting lost in the character," Cox says. "He said he had seen it before."

Protesting his innocence, he nevertheless left town. Until the end of the year he stayed in the area, taking hospitality from friends in Roswell, Carrizozo and other places. Then he went to Florida for two months. But last March he returned to Lincoln.

This time, however, he could not tell if he was completely welcome. Jack Rigney seemed glad to see him, he says, and talked of reviving the Billy the Kid act in July and August. But there was no open invitation to stay in his house in the meantime. And while the deputy sheriff was friendly at first, he soon returned to inquire about an apparent break-in at a Lincoln hotel, in a room once occupied by Billy the Kid.

Not quite knowing what to make of all this, Cox "fled to Albuquerque" for several weeks, to figure out what to do. He really does want, he says, to go back to Lincoln this summer and portray the Kid one more season before leaving the legendary gunfighter behind and getting on with his own life. Yet, if the atmosphere does not seem right, he does have a backup plan.

"If worse comes to worst," he says, "I'll go to Fort Sumner."

Article courtesy of Richard McCord

Derrell told Billy about Allen who was a farmer and rancher. Allen owned the Ft. Sumner lumber yard. So, Billy went to see the man about a job. Allen told Billy that he could not believe they were actually meeting because he had heard so much about him. The kid asked him if what he heard was good or bad. "Both", Allen replied. Billy told Allen that he was a good person and that he did not do any of the things he was being accused of in Lincoln county. Allen told the kid he would be safe there. Allen soon put Billy to work in the lumber yard. After work Allen took Billy to his dad's ranch. His father's name was Jake. Jake walked over to Billy with both of his arms extended to shake his hands.

Allen and The Kid farming in Fort Sumner, NM

138

A favorite hang out of The Kid's and his friends

"So, your Billy the Kid. It's nice to meet you", Jake said. Billy told Jake that he wanted to work and make some money. Jake had plenty of work to be done. Jake was known all over the state for his organic watermelons. They were irrigated from the Pecos River, which flows right through Ft. Sumner. Jake also grew alfalfa, hay, okra, tomatoes and cantaloupe. His son David was in charge of the chicken and ostrich farm. Billy met Jake's wife Leona who cooked every meal from their crops. Jake asked Billy if he could drive a tractor. Billy could not. Jake was willing to teach the kid. They headed down to one of his fields to get it ready to plant. After plowing all day it was time for supper. Around the dinner table sat the kid, Big Bill, David, Allen and Leona. Big Bill was married to Jake's daughter who was also a foreman and made sure everything ran smoothly when Jake was away. Two Mexican men named Fernando and Augustine also worked at the farm. They stayed in the bunk house out back.

Jake, Fernando and Augustine

After a couple of weeks of farming Billy went to visit Joe in the valley in Old Ft. Sumner near the Pecos River. Joe not only owned a store in Taiban, but he also operated another store and museum next to the cemetery where William H. Bonney, Charlie Bowdre and Tom O'Folliard were buried. Billy would sometimes stop and check for mail that would be forwarded in from Lincoln.

Post Office, Museum and Billy the Kid Outlaw Gang hang out

Joe also had a house in Ruidoso where he met Billy about a year ago at the fiesta. Billy and Joe headed over to Jake's ranch. Jake was there with his two brothers, Red and Clyde who fought in WWII. All of them owned land and cattle. Joe said hello and so did Jake and Red but Clyde turned his head and walked away towards David who was feeding his chickens. Billy felt the tension between Joe and Clyde but neither one of them would talk about it. Jake later told Billy it was just an old family problem that happened a long time ago between Joe and Clyde's families. Jake and Billy went to go get some hay. They went to get the stack wagon to get the hay so that Big Bill and Allen could take some to area ranchers. Jake had to take a tractor to the Pena's to be fixed uptown in Ft. Sumner. On the way up there Jake told Billy that Ft. Sumner has it's annual Old Ft. Sumner days in June so it was just around the corner. When it arrived the town was full of people who came as far as Puerto de Luna, Santa Rosa, Clovis, Roswell and San Juan. There were people dancing and participating in cow patty tossing contests. There was a tombstone race in which money was to be won. There was also plenty of Spanish and Anglo American food being served. People would come up to Billy and hug him. Spanish women were giving Billy roses and telling him that god had sent him to their town. The fiesta went on for a couple of days and it was a lot of fun. Later it was back to work at Jake's ranch. The watermelons were coming along. They were planted weeks back and were growing quite nicely. Allen and Billy the kid usually went together to feed the pigs which were Allen's pigs but they stayed on Jake's land. One day Allen was busy at the store and he told the kid to go and feed the pigs. As Billy approached the gate to go get the feed which was in the barn the pigs started charging at the gate. They wanted their food. Billy thought they wanted to make a meal out of him. He got nervous about the situation so to avoid opening the gate he climbed through a window to get inside the barn. Once the kid got the feed and climbed back out the window he proceeded to put the feed over the fence into the pigs feeding area. All of the pigs came running over like they were crazy and they started to eat. Billy quickly ran to the gate so that he could put the feed in all of the other pigs troths. Unfortunately, the pigs ate faster than the kid could move and they all came crashing at him and the bag of feed. Billy was able to get the feed into some of the troths before making it safely back to the barn. The pigs were still ramming against the barn door. Billy dropped the feed and said "Screw this". He then climbed out the window and headed back to Jake's ranch. However, Billy forgot to lock the barn door. Later Billy and Jake had to go chop the weeds around the watermelon crops. They were there for a few hours when it became sundown. It was dinner time. David, Allen, Big Bill and Jake were sitting around the table. As Billy came in it got very quiet. Jake looked at Allen and he looked back at Jake. Jake asked the kid if he forgot anything at the barn earlier that day. Allen was trying not to laugh. The kid told Jake that he did not believe there was anything that he had forgot to do. The kid told everyone that the pigs really gave him a lot of trouble. Jake told Billy that somehow the pigs were able to bust the door to the barn open and ransacked the place. All of the bags of feed had been torn into. Area farmers had to call Allen and let him know what was going on. The kid just put his head down feeling bad and told Jake that he was sorry. He said that he must have forgotten to lock the door. Jake told Billy that it was ok and that everyone makes mistakes. Everyone got a good laugh out of it.

Allen, Buck and Billy went to do some farming for a few hours. It got really hot at about one hundred and five degrees. It was a very dry heat and they had to drink a lot of water. After farming Allen had to take a truck full of hay to a ranch in Guadeloupe.

On the way to Guadeloupe with some hay

The kid and Buck went to help out. Guadeloupe was about twenty five miles from Ft. Sumner. After unloading the hay Billy saw some old ruins and decided to hide. Allen couldn't see where Billy had gone. Billy then peeked his head outside an old doorway and looked at everybody. Allen took Billy's picture to capture the moment.

The kid in Guadeloupe, NM

Then they headed back to Ft. Sumner. A few days later Billy went to the museum near the cemetery to visit Joe and check his mail. He was looking at the old pictures on the wall when he noticed two Lincoln county rangers had walked in. Billy dropped to the floor and he could see them walking and looking around. As Billy peered over the counter, he noticed that one of the rangers was his friend Manny.

He thought they had came to mess with him because of the news story that came out. Manny told Billy not to worry. They were coming from a meeting in Santa Fe and were passing through on their way back to Lincoln. Dee who was the other ranger told Billy that some of the political figures in Lincoln were a little upset when the news story came out and that it made the town look bad. Billy told Dee "What about me and those accusations that made me look bad? Unfortunately, certain people took the extra steps to accuse me of stealing and shooting cattle so I took the extra steps to publicly slap Lincoln in the face. I meant for them to take it face down. If they didn't like it, that's tough, because that's life". Dee just turned and walked away. Manny on the other hand shook Billy's hand and smiled. He told Billy that it was good seeing him again. Billy told Manny to tell Jack that he said hello and to tell him to give him a visit in old Ft. Sumner sometime. It was July of 1991 and the kid was staying busy. He was either helping Allen at the lumberyard or helping David with the chickens but he mainly spent his time helping Fernando, Augustine, Jake, Big Bill, Buck, Derrell and Joe get the watermelons ready. On one day after work Billy went to the museum to visit Joe who wasn't there but instead he was in Taiban. So Billy went to the cemetery out back to look around. Billy looked through the cage where William H. Bonney was buried. He looked down at the gravestone with sadness.

Billy no longer behind bars in Old Fort Sumner, NM

When he looked up he saw a beautiful blonde headed lady standing in front of him. She smiled and asked him if he came here a lot. Billy replied "I've been here once before". The lady introduced herself as Maureen and told the kid that he must be Billy. "The one and only", he said. Maureen asked Billy if he wanted to go to dinner. Billy accepted. After dinner Maureen and Billy went to the ranch where she was visiting. She was only visiting in Ft. Sumner for a few days and then it was off to Lincoln for another few days. She told Billy that she hoped he would visit her there as well. After hanging out for a few hours with Maureen, Billy headed back to Jake's ranch for some shut eye. At three o'clock in the morning Allen came to Billy's room and said "Kid, some of Jake's cattle got out. We need your help". The kid grabbed his hat and gun and quickly left with Allen. The cattle got out just east of Ft. Sumner. Allen's friend Joe came to help out along with David who joined in too. After finally rounding up

Billy and Maureen

the cattle and putting them back on the right land, it was back to the casa for some more shut eye. Later Billy got up for breakfast and then headed to the fields with Jake for a few hours of hoeing weeds around the watermelon plants. Jake was in his sixty's and still working the fields and going strong. The watermelons were coming along and getting bigger.

After work Maureen would meet Billy in the cemetery so they could talk. After visiting for a while, Maureen slipped Billy one hundred dollars in a gold clip and told him to keep it if he wanted. The money sure came in handy. Billy kissed her and thanked her. Maureen went back to the ranch and invited Billy back but he had to get up early for some farming and ranch work so he headed over to Jake's. The next day Billy and Allen took some hay to a near by ranch to drop off the bails. Then they headed over to Vaughn to drop off some hay there too. After that they headed back to the lumberyard in Ft. Sumner. After work Billy saw Maureen walking downtown. Billy told Allen that he would be right back and ran over to see Maureen for a visit. Maureen told Billy that she was leaving for Lincoln in a couple of hours and said that she would be staying at the Wortley Hotel in room number five. Billy told her that he would come visit her there. After finishing up in the lumberyard he headed over to Jake's for dinner.

The Lumberyard in Fort Sumner, NM

Jake, Leona and friends in Fort Sumner, NM

Jake had to take some hay into the Hondo Valley. Billy asked Jake if he could drop him off in Lincoln after they unloaded the hay. Jake asked Billy if he was going to see that lady. Billy answered yes. Jake told him that the lady was going to get him into trouble and that Lincoln was not the best place for the kid to be right now. Billy asked Jake to drop him off at Manny's casa just west of Lincoln. He would wait until nightfall and then follow the Rio Bonito until he came up behind the Wortley. Billy knew that Glen and Kay didn't own the hotel anymore and that the new owners were not fans of his according to what he had heard from his friends. Everybody at the dinner table discussed the trip and it was a go for tomorrow. Afterwards everyone went to their rooms and told each other goodnight. When morning came Jake and the kid headed towards Roswell and then west to the Hondo Valley to drop off the hay to several of the ranchers.

After a hard days work in the Hondo area Jake and the kid went over to Manny's casa where they had some New Mexico style chili with homemade flour tortillas. Joe was there too. Joe told Billy that he was pretty slick with what he had pulled with the newspapers and going to Ft. Sumner. The kid told him what goes around comes around and then he started laughing. Joe told Billy to eat up and that he was safe there. He told Billy to forget about the political jug heads that were giving him trouble. After dinner Jake headed back to Ft. Sumner and the kid stayed in Lincoln.

Billy farmed and ranched this area in Ft. Sumner, NM

Later that night Billy went down to the Rio Bonito and followed the river eastward towards Lincoln. Once the kid was behind the Wortley, he took the trail through the woods and came up right behind the hotel and went to room number five. Billy knocked on the door and Maureen welcomed him in. She had some music playing and candles lit all around the room. Billy and Maureen danced for hours and after being intimate with each other they drifted off to sleep. When morning came Billy jumped into the bath tub. He just relaxed in the tub while smoking a cigar. Maureen asked Billy to come back with her to Calgary. "It gets cold in Calgary, doesn't it?" asked Billy. She told Billy that it did sometimes get cold there. She told him that her father would hook him up with a good job. Billy knew he wasn't going to leave New Mexico, but felt bad that he would not be going with her. Maureen started to cry a little but she understood. As Billy got dressed and combed his hair back he leaned over to Maureen and gave her a kiss. He wished her a safe trip back. He had spent three days in Lincoln with Maureen before he had to leave. He walked off the Wortley Hotel porch waving goodbye and smoking his cigar. The owner of the Wortley came walking by and saw Billy but seemed a little nervous to walk by him. Billy blew smoke from his mouth that drifted overtop the owners head. The owner told Billy good morning while keeping his head down. Billy just smiled and said "Top of the morning to you sir". When nobody else was in sight Billy disappeared behind the hotel and headed to the trail through the woods to the Rio Bonito. He headed east until he was behind Tunstall's Store. Billy just waited behind the store until he saw Leroy driving the mail route. He stopped at the post office at the store. As Leroy grabbed his bags of mail he looked up and saw that the kid was back. Billy smiled and nodded at Leroy. Leroy knew that meant he needed a ride. Billy slipped into the van and out of Lincoln. No one had noticed what was going on. Leroy asked Billy why he was in Lincoln. Billy said that he met this beautiful lady in Ft. Sumner and she had came into Lincoln for a few days. So he just had to go there. Leroy just started laughing. After talking for a while, Leroy dropped Billy off in Roswell.

The Valley in Fort Sumner, NM

Billy went over to Tom's ranch to hang out for a while but needed to get back to Jake's to help out on the ranch. Jake and the kid took some hay to Puerto de Luna. Later they went to visit Victor and had lunch. Jake and Billy went back to Ft. Sumner to check on the watermelons which were coming along really well. Fernando, Augustine and the kid were busy hoeing the weeds. Jake went to check on the tomatoes, okra and other fields. Jake then picked up Billy so they could get some hay on the stack wagon. Jake was driving the stack wagon while Billy sat on a bar out in the open away from the driver. Jake told Billy when the flat bed was half full he would stop the stack wagon so the kid could cross tie. Jake told Billy not to step on a switch in the middle of the flat bed because it would trip the switch and would cause the flat bed to start going up. The kid went to cross tie and was looking for the switch to make sure he didn't step on it. It wasn't until he moved his foot that he realized he had been standing on the switch. Billy looked at Jake and yelled "Oh shit!" The flat bed started to go up. All Billy could do was hang on.

The Stack Wagon

The kid looked over the front and decided to drop on the chain and try to move out of the way fast. Jake grabbed Billy by the belt on his pants and yanked him out of the way. The flat bed came slamming down just missing the kid. Fernando and Augustine were also waiting on Jake and the kid to bring the hay to the truck to unload. They both saw what happened to Billy and thought that he was going to be killed. Jake told everyone that the kid moved as quick as a cat. Jake also told everyone that he messed his pants from fright because there had been a lot of people killed on stack wagons. The kid was lucky to have survived. Billy just started laughing and everyone looked at him like he was crazy. Ken, Donna and the boys were coming from Roswell and decided to stop and visit with Billy. Ken told Billy they were on their way to Farmington to see a friend and said that the kid was welcomed to go with them if he wanted to. Billy told Ken that he would love to go for the ride. Billy let Jake know that he would be gone for a week. Billy was glad to spend time with Ken and his family. It was hot and dry in Farmington. This was Indian territory.

Billy riding off on the Indian Reservation

Ken found his friend and they stopped in for a visit. Billy, Dennis, Brian, Shannon, Tim and Mathew went outside to hang on the ranch. Then all of the sudden they heard someone yelling. An Indian on a horse came riding up to them. Billy and the boys just looked at each other with concern. The Indian just rode his horse in a circle around the boys while looking at them and speaking in a native tongue. The horse stopped and the Indian was looking dead at Billy. The Indian introduced himself as Herald, a Navajo Indian. He asked Billy if he was Billy the Kid. Billy replied "No, my name is William H. Cox II from Ft. Sumner, NM. Herald told Billy he knew who he was because he had read about him. He started laughing as he got off of his horse to shake Billy's hand. He then told Billy that Ken had come to visit his grandfather. Ken used to live in Farmington and Donna used to work there. He also told Billy to come with him because he wanted to show him an old hang out where outlaws, lawmen and Indians would hide out.

Billy and Herald at the Indian Reservation

Herald and his friends would party at this spot. It was about ten miles away from the ranch and out in the middle of nowhere. Herald asked Billy if he believed in the spirit world. Billy told him that he did. Once they arrived at the canyon Billy was really amazed at it. Herald told Billy that nobody could find this canyon. Herald said that his people had been coming here for centuries and that this was their land. Herald told the kid that he was always welcomed there and that he would consider him family. Billy thanked Herald for his kind gesture. Then Herald put a small rock out in the open. He grabbed his Winchester and went target shooting with Billy to see who was the best shot. Herald blew the rock all to pieces. After the target shooting Herald and Billy went back to the ranch for dinner. Donna was helping in the kitchen while Ken and the boys were telling Herald's grandfather ghost stories. The next day Herald's grandfather let Billy take his horse for a ride on the open range. After a couple of days of roaming that part of New Mexico Billy, Ken, Donna and the boys said goodbye and headed back to Ft. Sumner.

Billy at the railroad depot in Vaughn, NM 1991

The family dropped Billy off at Jake's ranch. Billy got right back into the swing of things at work. The watermelons were coming along and it would be no time before they would be ready to pick. It was August of 1991 and Billy was staying busy on the ranch. Billy C and Gary had been hanging out in Ft. Sumner lately. They told Billy that the Lincoln annual fiesta, better known as Lincoln days, was coming up this weekend. They thought it would be good to take a ride down there and make a cameo appearance. Gary and Billy C had a friend with them from Carrizozo. The kid had a plan for when they arrived in Lincoln just in case Deputy Mac wanted to start some trouble with him. The kid knew that Mac didn't know Billy C and Gary's friend so it was possible to bluff him into thinking their friend was a lawyer. Billy knew that the heat would be on in Lincoln but he had to show them that he's still around and that they failed with their deceit. Buck wanted to go with the kid and his friends. Billy contacted Tom from Roswell and told him about the plan and asked him to meet them in Lincoln that weekend. Billy had some work to make up for before he left for Lincoln. Gary and Billy C, along with their friend Terry had been camping out at Stinking Springs for the last two weeks. Jake let them clean up and join them for dinner. All the work was in check and the kid was ready to head to Lincoln with his friends for the fiesta. It was the first weekend in August and the kid, Gary, Billy C and Terry arrived in Lincoln around eleven o'clock in the morning. The people were partying up and down on the only street in town. The kid's plan was when Mac drove by and gave him grief he would look down at Terry and would have a notepad and a pen ready pretending to write down information. As the kid, Gary, Billy and Terry walked down the main street Tom was hanging out near Tunstall's Store and he joined in the walk. Then unexpectedly Ken, Brian, Dennis, Shannon and Jack joined in the walk to show support for the kid. Manny and Jack waved at the kid. Joe was there and smiling at the kid. As they walked down the street towards the courthouse the kid said good afternoon to Raflita. She asked Billy how he had been. Billy replied "I've been living and working in Ft. Sumner". Dustin, Tim, Kevin, Harvey and Darla were standing out in front of their general store waving at Billy. Sure enough Deputy Mac came up fast and drove by the kid and his friends. As he drove by he picked up his CB radio and started to talk or look like he was talking to someone. At that same time the kid looked at Terry who started to pretend to write things down on his notepad. Then Mac turned around and drove back by with the radio in hand while looking at Billy. Terry continued steady with the bluff while looking back at Mac. This spooked Mac because he didn't know who Terry was. He figured he may be some sort of legal advisor. The bluff had worked and Mac was very careful with his actions from then on with the kid. Buck was in the alley next to Tunstall's Store. "You don't think I'd let you come into Lincoln without me, did you kid?" asked Buck. He went to join the kid. Blake and Patrick were playing their music by the Wortley Hotel. The kid started his own party right in the middle of Lincoln. Scott came over to join the fun. Everybody was laughing and pointing at Mac who could only stand there and watch with his other deputies. Mac did not know what to make out of this situation. Billy yelled out to Mac and said "Hey, when are you going to get with the new program?" Mac did not respond. After having fun at the fiesta for several hours it was time for Billy to head back to Ft. Sumner. As he left he clinched his Winchester and waived it in the air while everyone watched him. "I'll be leaving now and going back to my home in Ft. Sumner where I work and perhaps I will see you again in the future", said Billy.

Early morning in Stinking Springs near Ft. Sumner

He then said adios to Lincoln. He had also seen his old friends Carolyn and Joe who had come in from their Roswell ranch. Joe was still working hard with his cattle. Joe and Carolyn told Billy to visit more often when in the Roswell area. Billy said bye to everybody. The kid and his friends moved fast out of Lincoln and back up to Ft. Sumner. He thanked everyone who supported him. Billy was back in Ft. Sumner and working with Jake. Jake told Billy that the watermelons were ready to be picked and he would be getting them ready for the Santa Fe market. Cantaloupes and a special melon called the "Jake Melon" would be taken to the market as well. When it rained in that part of New Mexico it really came a down pour. Later that evening when everyone got off from their jobs they went to the watermelon fields to help Jake pick. Allen, the kid, Joe, Big Bill, Buck, Jake and David once had to pick about three hundred watermelons at night in the rain until about two o'clock in the morning. All Billy and the boys did while they picked melons was sing and act crazy while cracking jokes on one another. It was a real good time. The rain wouldn't stop and finally when the boys were done picking the melons everybody headed back to their casa to get some sleep.

Old Fort Sumner, NM

Jake and Billy had to get up at four o'clock in the morning to haul the melons one hundred and eighty miles away from Ft. Sumner to the mountains of Santa Fe. Jake drove up to the out skirts of Las Vegas, New Mexico, then onto the old Santa Fe trail which is a highway. This route took Jake and the kid straight to the market. As they pulled into the market place they saw the press waiting on the arrival of Jake and his sweet organic watermelons. "Who's your helper?" asked a member of the press. "I dug him out of the ground in Ft. Sumner. This is our modern day Billy the Kid", said Jake. Before Jake could get another word out the people flocked to the truck for a watermelon which sold at two dollars a piece. Even the other vendors would look over at Jake's truck and trailer with envy. After a couple of hours of selling watermelons there were only about fifty melons left. Jake and the kid went to a fancy restaurant named "La Tortilla" in Santa Fe. Jake would always bring the restaurant a couple melons. Jake treated the kid to lunch there. After eating and visiting with the work crew at the restaurant Jake and the kid had to get rid of those melons so they drove to area organic supermarkets that already carried Jake's melons and some of them even had a life size picture of Jake holding his melons in the produce department.

Jake and The Kid selling watermelons in Santa Fe

Jake was able to unload the rest of the melons. Then they headed back to Ft. Sumner. On the way back just south of Las Vegas, New Mexico, Jake asked Billy if he wanted something to drink. Billy said yes. Jake turned down this old highway that took them to the small village of Anton Chico which had a general store where they stopped for a soda. Later they came to an old Route 66 town named Santa Rosa just ten miles from Puerto de Luna. They finally made their way back to the ranch and called it a night after what was a very long day. Early morning came fast and it was straight to the alfalfa fields to cut the hay and then bail it. Then the kid would go help Fernando and Augustine hoe the weeds around the watermelons. The kid went to pick some tomatoes and okra and later headed out for lunch. After lunch Billy would go help Allen at the lumber yard. One afternoon Big Bill came to the lumberyard to get the kid, Fernando and Augustine so that they could pick two hundred watermelons, one hundred cantaloupes and fifty of Jake's special melons. It was hard work but everyone worked together and got the job done very quickly. On the way back to Jake's ranch, the kid decided to ride with Allen and would follow Big Bill, Fernando and Augustine with their load of melons. Billy wanted to stop at the museum to check his mail and say hi to everyone. That put them way behind the others. After Billy checked his mail he jumped back in the truck with Allen and proceeded to catch up with the others. When they finally came up on the others their truck was stopped in the middle of the road and surrounded by the sheriff's department which were pointing guns at them. Allen and the kid just looked at each other with shock and concern. They stopped their truck as a precaution. According to the sheriff's department some saddles and other horse equipment were stolen from a nearby ranch near Jake's ranch. Also a gun was stolen. Someone had fired the stolen gun causing a stray bullet to go through a kitchen window and into a wall. The sheriff found footprints that led them to the bunk house behind Jake's casa where Fernando and Augustine were living. This meant that the two boys were responsible for the crime. They had been drinking all night and were drunk when they stole the stuff. They were arrested and Jake cursed them in Spanish for doing this to him.

The old cemetery in Old Fort Sumner, NM

Jake had taken good care of them and paid them well and gave them a free place to stay. Fernando and Augustine were sent back to Mexico. Later at Jake's ranch, Big Bill came out with new pants on. Allen asked Big Bill what happened to his old ones. Big Bill told everyone that he had to throw them away. He wished he had not been driving the truck that had Fernando and Augustine in it. Days later Allen and the kid took some hay to Puerto de Luna and then they brought some to Corona. Tuesdays and Thursdays were the days that Jake and the kid would head to Santa Fe with the watermelons. Allen, Buck, David, Joe and the kid went to Guadeloupe to visit Allen's friend on his ranch. Allen's friend had several head of cattle and was selling a couple of them. Jake was interested in buying them. Allen's friend invited everyone to dinner where he talked some business over with Allen. After they ate, the boys went over to Joe's ranch not far from Guadeloupe. Joe took everybody to the famous Rosie's Cantina that sits right on the Pecos River. Joe's great grandfather built the building during the late 1800's. It was built so the family could hang out or have dances and parties. Joe had it fixed up nice with a saloon look. It was a great place to have a couple of drinks and relax while overlooking the river. The kid asked Joe how the place got it's name. Joe and Allen asked Billy if he ever met Rosie. "Who the hell is Rosie?" asked the kid. "Hell, we have to introduce you to Rosie", said Joe and Allen while laughing. They told Billy that Rosie was in the back room waiting for him.

Near Taiban, NM

Billy slowly walked to the door while laughing quietly. "Go ahead Billy, she's waiting for you", said Allen. As Billy slowly opened the door he saw that it was dark so he turned on the light. They had tricked Billy. On the wall behind the bed was an old picture of a full size women in a short dress wearing old looking boots. She was holding a bottle of whiskey. "You guys are crazy", said the kid. Everyone began drinking and listening to good old country music. Billy asked Joe if he had any Garth Brooks. "Sure, Billy, I have some friends in low places", said Joe. Before they knew it the time was about three o'clock in the morning. Some of the boys decided to sleep at the cantina. Joe walked to his home were his wife was. Allen went back to Ft. Sumner to see his wife. Buck drank until he passed out on the floor. David fell asleep on a bed roll. Billy went to sleep next to Rosie in her cantina.

Guadeloupe, NM

Joe came into the cantina early at about seven o'clock in the morning and threw water on Buck and told everyone to get up and get ready for work. There were cattle to work on his ranch that day. Joe asked where Billy was. Buck started laughing and said that Billy was with Rosie. Joe opened the door and there was the kid lying in bed and snoring. Joe woke him up and said there was work to be done. Joe had put some coffee on. Allen showed up with his dad Jake to help Joe with his cattle. Joe's cattle was in the wrong area and had to be moved to another area suitable for grazing. Allen and Joe had Buck and the kid on top of a hill and told them that they were going to drive the cattle toward them and they didn't want the cattle to get off of the trail. So, when Buck and the kid saw the cattle coming down the trail they started yelling at them in order to make them stay on coarse. Jake, Joe and Allen went to round up the cattle and bring them down the trail. Buck and the kid waited about forty-five minutes for the cattle. They heard the cattle coming down below but when the cattle came around the corner fast the kid and Buck started to yell, however it was not loud enough. The cattle started to spread out everywhere. Buck and the kid tried to organize them but it was to late. Joe and Allen were on horseback and were a little upset with Buck and the kid. Joe was understanding and knew that things happened. The cattle had a mind of their own. Joe, Allen, Jake, Buck and the kid had to round up all of the cattle which took several hours to do. They finally got the cattle where they needed to be. When the day was done they were all tired and hungry. After dinner Buck stayed at Joe's ranch to help out for a few more days. The kid rode back with Allen, David and Jake to Ft. Sumner. David got dropped off at a little building near downtown across the street from a museum based mainly on Billy the Kid. The little building is where David had a fruit and veggie stand. Allen went to the lumberyard to do some paperwork. When Jake and the kid went to the ranch Jake told Billy to take David some melons. The kid drove Jake's old 1957 Chevy truck. When the kid arrived at David's fruit stand to drop off the melons David told Billy to drop them off on the other side of the building.

The Church in Guadeloupe, NM

Billy decided to put the truck in reverse and back around the building to the other side. But, as he turned his head around he backed up to see his driver side door was open. All of the sudden the door hit a tree causing the door to come completely off. Billy slammed on the brakes and David came running over. They both looked at each other and said "Oh shit!" Old Jake wasn't going to like this one. David rode with the kid back to Jake's ranch to help him break the news. Billy told Jake about the door and thought Jake was going to get real mad. Sure enough, Jake did get mad. Leona, David, Buck and Big Bill just laughed. Jake told David and Billy to get in and get ready for dinner. August was just about over and here crept September just around the corner. The melons were keeping everyone including the kid very busy. One day Billy was hoeing the weeds and picking okra and tomatoes. He was also working with the hay. Billy wasn't drinking enough water that day and to make matters worse he was wearing a black survival vest.

Cerrillos, NM

After work was done for the day Billy met up with everyone for dinner. Afterwards the kid was beat, so he decided to relax in a rocking chair. Billy started to have a cold sweat and felt nervous and weak as if he could pass out. Jake realized that there was something wrong and that Billy had gotten to much sun. Jake got a cool rag to put over Billy's head and made the kid lie down. Leona got Billy some water to drink. It was a mild heat stroke but Jake thought it might get worse and they may need to call a doctor. Billy was tough. He fought through it and after a few hours started to feel better. Billy took the next day off to rest. He rode on an old fashioned bike that belonged to Jake. Billy rode the bike to the other side of Ft. Sumner to visit a friend who lived on a ranch just outside of the town. The ranch was near Sunnyside Springs. The kid visited with the family and took the kid on a hike to the Pecos River. Later the family invited the kid for dinner. The kid talked about ranch work at Jake's and that he was really enjoying it. There was always plenty of work to do and Billy really felt like part of the family. It was getting late so the kid started to ride back to Jake's ranch in the valley. Billy got back to the ranch and while getting ready for bed he realized that his necklace, which had an anchor made from gold on it, had came off during the bike ride. Billy finally found his anchor charm but not his gold chain. So Billy grabbed a lantern and retraced his route back to the ranch. As he rode through the desert he heard a pop sound in the distance. As he got closer to the ranch he heard another pop sound. Seconds later Billy heard the high pitch whistle of a bullet fly right next to him. Billy didn't know where the bullet came from but he wasn't going to stick around and find out. Billy turned that bike around and hauled ass back to Jake's. Billy was riding so fast he could feel his heart pounding and his adrenaline was pumping. As he came into the neighborhoods of Ft. Sumner he realized that his lantern was still on and thought he was a lighted target. He nervously tried to turn it off. Right as he turned the lantern off he slammed into a curb and his body flew through the air and he landed on his back. The kid left the lantern and jumped on his bike continuing to haul ass. In this time the kid was sweating and could feel the wetness on his sleeves. At first he thought the wetness on his sleeve meant he could have been shot. Billy was really in shock as he came into town where there were lights. He could see his shoulder and realized it was just sweat. Billy continued to ride back towards Jake's place. "Screw the necklace", Billy thought. He had a tough time sleeping for a few days. He could not stop thinking about how close the bullet had come to hitting him and making him the dead kid in Ft. Sumner. A few days later it was work on the farm as usual. Jake and the kid were still going to Santa Fe to sell watermelons twice a week. Billy put some turquoise beads on a leather string with his anchor charm making a new and improved necklace. It was September now and it was starting to get a little cool outside. Billy C and Gary were back in the Ft. Sumner area camping out. Allen needed the kid's help in the lumberyard for a few days. After work Billy and Allen would go get the stack wagon to get hay. Billy stayed real busy in the month of September. There was no time to take off. Gary and Billy C would come to help out with the melons. In late September 1991 Tom came up from Roswell to see Billy for a moment.

Golden, NM

"Good to see you, Rudy", said Billy. Billy asked him to take a walk. Kneeling down on the other side of the building eating potatoes and burritos, the kid looked down at them and said "Did you bring those burritos from Ft. Sumner and did you bring me one too?" Gary looked up with a mouthful of food and wondered who had just asked him that. As soon as he looked up and realized who it was, everyone started laughing. Gary and Billy C got up and joined the kid. Billy C was smoking his pipe as usual. Rudy, Buck, Gary, Billy C and the kid were hanging out at the Grzelachowski house where William H. Bonney had his last Christmas dinner while he was on his way to Santa Fe during his incarceration. Billy turned around and saw a figure on a horse coming his way. As he got closer Billy thought the fellow looked familiar. When the figure got even closer Billy began to smile and told the boys it was sheriff James of Lincoln county. "Do you like him, Billy?" asked Buck. "Yes, he is my friend and a damn good sheriff", said Billy. James told Billy he had heard that the kid was in the Ft. Sumner area. Billy told him that he had been in Ft. Sumner ever since the problems in Lincoln. "You don't think I would miss this fiesta and reenactment do you"? Billy asked.

Billy C and Gary at the Puerto de Luna fiesta

James told Billy that it was good to see him and offered to buy him a drink. As they walked into the general store James asked Billy what he wanted to drink. "Water", the kid replied. Billy asked what brought James to Puerto de Luna. He told Billy that Joe of Taiban, who was the president of the Billy the Kid Outlaw Gang club, invited him there to be sheriff during the reenactment. Billy thought that was very cool. It was crowded with people coming from surrounding areas. Soon a wagon came up with Buck, Gary, Billy C, Rudy and Tom with shackles and handcuffs. James was twirling a handcuff and telling Billy to come up there with them because there could not be a reenactment without him. Billy smiled and jumped into the wagon. The reenactment was historical. The sheriff of Lincoln county, James, brought in the outlaws on a horse drawn wagon. They came down the old trail that went right in front of the Grzelachowski store, saloon and jail. Joe from Taiban, Johnny from Clovis and two other deputies led the posse while Billy the kid stood up and the other outlaws sat down. All of their legs were shackled and handcuffed together while the kid shouted to the people "It was a war. I took from the rich and gave to the poor".

The Grzelachowski home and saloon in Puerto de Luna

Billy the kid attends a local fiesta in Puerto de Luna

San Juan, NM Amphitheater

Senator Pete came to see the reenactment. Soon after, the fiesta came and their was plenty of food and music. Stan came all the way from Alburg to see the boys and was a very good friend of the kid's. Joe and other members of the outlaw gang put a historical state marker at the site. Politicians from Santa Fe came down to recognize the event while Billy danced with the senoritas and was having nothing but fun. Gary and Buck were dancing with the ladies too. Rudy had a beautiful Spanish lady from Santa Rosa. German television was there doing a documentary and filmed the event. Yugoslavian television was also there. American television was there, not to mention the newspapers were there too recording this historical event. As the fiesta was drawing near the end Billy the kid, Buck, Gary and Billy C were riding out of Puerto de Luna and heading back to Ft. Sumner. The boys took the back way there. They went over Coronado's bridge and headed east. Billy was back at the ranch and working for Jake. October was coming to an end.

Jake, Billy, Allen, Big Bill, David and Leona at the dinner table

Stan in Albuquerque, NM 1991

172

Puerto de Luna, NM 1991

Gary and Billy in Puerto de Luna, NM 1991

Victor in Puerto de Luna, NM 1991

Johnny, Bill, Gary and Billy on the Pecos River

Puerto de Luna, NM 1991

Joe came to visit Billy in Ft. Sumner. Joe let Billy know that there was a dedication over at Texico and the House of Representatives and the governor of New Mexico would be there. They all
wanted Billy to be there. Billy took this ride by himself to meet the governor. Billy arrived at
the end of October in Texico where the dedication took place. Miss New Mexico was there too.
Billy just hung around and ate the food. Everybody just shook Billy's hand and introduced
themselves to him. Soon a helicopter came in and landed. It was governor Bruce King of New
Mexico. He shook Billy's hand and thanked him for all he had done for the state. The governor
also shook hands with the other attendees and thanked them for their contributions. After the
dedication Billy went back to Ft. Sumner quickly to help Jake. Soon it was November and it
was getting cold. The watermelons were busy this year. Irrigating off the Pecos River was exciting and hard work, but it was also a lot of fun. Watermelons, cantaloupes and other melons
were all slowing down for the year. Sometimes there were light snow storms but they were not
real bad ones. Jake and the kid took some hay to Yeso to a ranch.

Guadalupe, NM, in 1991

Billy the kid was staying busy with the hay and helping Allen at the lumberyard through most of the month of November. Gary and Billy C had been hanging out at the White Oaks Saloon talking with Jim, who owned the saloon. Mostly they talked about business. The kid was also laying low in Ft. Sumner mainly because of the cold season. There was a big dinner at Jake's house and Leona cooked a beautiful Thanksgiving meal for everyone. December came rolling up and winter was going strong. Gary and Billy C came up from Carrizozo and went to set up camp at Stinking Springs. Then they went into Ft. Sumner to see Billy. Gary found Billy at Ft. Sumner and told him that he had a business deal for him. Gary asked the kid if he wanted to sell Christmas Trees in Tucson, Arizona for a few weeks. Jim in White Oaks had a brother in Michigan who owned a cherry business and a Christmas tree business. Gary told Billy that they would pay him eight hundred dollars to help sell the trees. The kid accepted and asked when he was to leave for the job.

Camping out on the way to Ft. Sumner in December

The van that flipped

Gary told Billy that they would need to leave the next day for Carrizozo and then leave for Arizona. The kid went to camp out at the spring with Gary and Billy C. It was fifteen degrees that night but the fire kept everyone warm. The thick bed rolls provided warmth as well. Morning came and Gary made coffee before heading out. Gary and the kid went to see Jim in White Oaks and to get the go ahead to start heading to Arizona. The trip was on, but before they took off Jim wanted to buy everyone drinks. "What are you going to have, kid?" asked Jim. "Water", replied the kid. Jim told Billy it was good to have him back in White Oaks. After a few drinks and after Gary had a couple of shots of whiskey, soon they were ready to go to Carrizozo to get ready for Arizona. As they left the saloon which was the old trail but was a paved and very winding road the kid and Gary got to talking. When they approached the last curve before the highway they were going too fast. All of the sudden they went off the road. They tried to pull back and went over the railroad tracks and the van rolled a couple of times and finally came to a stop right side up. Thinking the van might blow up, the kid jumped out the front windshield and slid down the hood while telling Gary to get out. Gary's window was half down so when the van rolled it broke the glass which cut Gary's ear half off. It was dark and they were out in the middle of the desert. The kid wrapped Gary's ear with an old shirt and they started walking through the desert heading to Carrizozo. Billy C stayed at the house and did not go with them to White Oaks. When Gary and the kid finally got to Carrizozo the kid took Gary to Leroy's ranch so Leroy's girlfriend could bandage Gary's ear better.

The curve coming out of White Oaks where Gary and Billy flipped the van

Leroy helped Gary and the kid that night and was a very loyal and true friend. The kid and Gary thanked him for his help. Then Gary and the kid went over to Gary's casa where Billy C was. Billy C was in shock but was relieved that they didn't get killed. The next day Gary had the van towed to the house and had to borrow one of Jim's other trucks to take to Arizona. The three headed to Arizona the next day. They had been driving for hours and somewhere near the border of New Mexico and Arizona the boys were tired and set up camp in the middle of the desert. In the morning Billy C was up early smoking his pipe and having a cup of coffee. The boys were up and continued the trip to Tucson. They finally made it to Tucson to the area where they were to sell the trees.

Camping out on the open range

Arizona 1991

The kid, Gary and Billy C met Walter, David and the pool shark, Jim. Billy C made some calls to the press to let them know that the kid was in town. Soon the kid was on the front page of the Tucson Citizen. The headline read "The Kid is Alive and Selling Christmas Trees at the Corner of Campbell and Grant". The business was on and doing great. Billy checked out old Tucson while he was there. People came to greet the kid. For two and a half weeks Billy helped to sell the trees and load them into people's cars. He also assisted in unloading the semi trucks when they came in. The Christmas tree adventure came to an end and Billy the kid got his eight hundred dollars in cash.

BILLY THE KID

is alive and well and selling Christmas trees at the corner of Campbell and Grant

By JULIE SZEKELY
Citizen Staff Writer

William H. Cox sat on a plastic ice chest, chomping on a Whataburger with cheese.

"If Billy the Kid were alive today," he was asked, "what would he eat for lunch?"

Cox's mouth stopped shut. Then, "Whatever's available, I guess," he said, continuing his chewing. "Whataburger."

Cox, 25, was taking a break from his current gig — selling Christmas trees — which brought him to Tucson from Fort Sumner, N.M.

Fort Sumner, as you may or may not know, is the final resting place of Billy the Kid, whose name was William H. Bonney. For the last two years, it also has been the home of Cox, who has taken on as his current adventure the re-roaming of Billy the Kid's old stomping grounds.

Cox's fascination with Billy the Kid began when he saw "Young Guns" in 1988 while living in Florida.

"The movie just blew my mind," he said, finishing his burger. "The scenery — that's what I was fascinated with, and the music — like something was fixin' to happen. I said, 'This really happened?' and my friend said, 'Yeah, it really happened.'"

A year went by. Cox started reading books such as "The Authentic Life of William H. Bonney."

"I started matching things up with names in the movie. Then I looked on a map and I seen Lincoln and Capitan and Fort Stanton and White Oaks, and I started thinking, 'Man, it's still there.' And I'd always heard out West it's still open wilderness, and I started thinking, 'I gotta go out there and do an adventure. I'll go out there and add it on to all my other adventures, like a ladder or something.'"

When he saw a hat just like the Kid's, he bought it. Then he took a bus to Roswell, N.M., for a two-week vacation.

"I got off the bus, and I was looking for some history, so I went to the local museum there and a man named Ken Hobbs — he's kinda a local historian there and he was a security guard — and I walked in and he just looked at me, and I told him I was from Florida and came to learn about the Kid, and he said, 'You look just like him.' I thought he was just influenced by the hat, and he said, 'We got to get you up to Lincoln.'"

It was in Lincoln County that Billy the Kid gained his reputation as a killer, avenging the death of John Tunstall, a man who "always treated

me fair," the Kid is rumored to have said.

Cox's new friend took him to Lincoln.

"I was all tripping out," Cox said. "This is where it all happened."

The town, population 70, has changed little in the 110 years since Billy the Kid's escapades.

Cox walked up to the courthouse — the same courthouse in which Billy the Kid was found guilty of murdering

Color photo by RICK WILEY/Tucson Citizen

William H. Cox, rifle at ready, strikes a pose similar to his hero, Billy the Kid.

William Brady, the sheriff who had deputized the posse of men who killed Tunstall.

Jack Rigney, chief ranger of Lincoln State Monuments, was there in the courthouse.

Before Cox could check out the courthouse, Rigney was snapping Polaroids of him standing next to a life-size photograph of the Kid.

"He just looked at me and said, 'You look just like him. There's no doubt in my mind that you'd win the lookalike contest. I've got to get some pictures of you.'"

"What's your name?" Rigney asked Cox. "Billy," Cox replied.

Rigney turned to some tourists, "Don't give this guy a gun," he told them.

When Cox returned to Florida, he took a copy of the Polaroid with him and began to look for his similarities to the Kid. "I started looking at the bone structure and the hair and I seen something there."

Intrigued, he started reading accounts of Billy the Kid.

"He was Irish, a Sagittarius, we both are William H., we both lost mothers at a young age. He was 15, I think; I was 13.

He decided to accept an invitation from Rigney to spend the next July and August at his home, and to compete in the next look-alike contest, and he began to prepare in earnest.

"I started studying that pose. I bought me a Winchester, a little .22, started hittin' that pose, identical. I'd just step right into it, just trying to please myself. Started studying his fingers, the way his fingers were resting, the way his shoulders were slunched down."

A year later, he set his backpack down in Rigney's house and stepped back out on Lincoln's main street.

"I started walking up and down the street and people started asking Jack, 'Who is this kid? He looks just like the Kid.'"

They'd take his picture, give him a tip.

"A couple bucks, some gave me five, some 10."

And he got names of people he might need to contact, "'cause I knew I was gonna be needin' work once tourist season ended, and people were sayin', 'You can stay with us.'"

Cox has been staying ever since with various friends he made during his first summer in Lincoln.

"I stay in the little towns — Lincoln, Carrizozo, Capitan, Roswell and Fort Sumner — with all the descendants of families that knew the Kid. I come in

THE KID's, continued/3B

Arizona awaits the Kid's arrival

The Kid's alive and selling trees here

Continued from 1B

and people just treat me nice like they treated the Kid back then. People in Fort Sumner hid him out from the sheriff — from Pat Garrett."

Part of Cox's adventure has been the assortment of odd jobs he's taken on to earn his keep.

"I wanted to kinda struggle," he said. "It'd be better that way.

Cox

"Doin' odd jobs to help people out — chopping wood, something the Kid woulda done, stack wood, build fences, repair fences, digging post holes. Whatever needs to be done. I come into their house and work for them and eat and, like, build a relationship with them."

He also has been taking in sights he believes were in the Kid's line of sight during his roamings, photographing and collecting memories along the way — "seeing the country where he was at, you know."

Similarities between William H. Bonney and William H. Cox

- Their names
- Both are Irish
- Both are Sagittarians
- Each lost his mother while in his teens
- Both were born on the East Coast — Bonney in New York City; Cox in Florida
- Cox is small in stature; so was Bonney
- Similar facial features

While other belongings remain in New Mexico, Cox carries his pictures and other mementos with him in a stack of photo albums, which he willingly displays.

He has no idea whether he's at the beginning, middle or end of the Billy the Kid adventure — "the plan is just work. Keep working, make money" — but Cox says it can't go on forever. The Kid was killed when he was 21; Cox turned 25 yesterday.

"I never thought I'd get old, but I'm gettin' older. I don't 25 though, do I? Or 24?"

185

Camping out on the way to Ft. Sumner, NM 1991

The kid, Gary and Billy C said goodbye and headed back to Carrizozo. It was a long ride but they finally arrived back in Carrizozo on December 23, 1991. The kid, Gary and Billy C had a small Christmas in Carrizozo at Gary's casa. They bought each other a small gift. It was snowing on Christmas night. Billy the kid got this feeling that the end was near. He didn't tell Gary or Billy C. The kid told them that he must get back to Ft. Sumner. They understood and told him to be careful and to have a good trip back. The kid told them that he was going to stop in Roswell to see Tom. The kid told them goodbye. He went to El Capitan and then took the route east to Roswell to avoid Lincoln. He arrived at Tom's ranch on December 26, 1991. The kid asked Tom if he wanted to take a ride to Ft. Sumner with a sad look on his face. Tom knew that the end was near and told the kid that he would go. Tom told his girlfriend that he would be back in a few days. Tom grabbed his rifle and packed his bag. He and the kid hit the road. Tom wanted to do some hog hunting along the way. Tom took an old ranch road that followed the Pecos River all the way to Ft. Sumner. The kid and Tom had been on this road many times in the past coming and going to Roswell and Ft. Sumner. While they slept in some abandoned rock homes from the 1800's, Billy rounded up some wood to make a cross and carved his name and the years that he roamed New Mexico. They decided to stay in this old home that Tom and Don stayed in a lot while they were on hunting trips. Tom and the kid went to the Pecos River to hide in the brush and hope to sneak up on a wild hog and kill it so that they could have din-

Tom looking for hogs on the Pecos River

Sure enough a hog came running out behind some brush and Tom shot and hit it right in the head. The boys watched the hog fall down. Tom cut up the meat while the kid got the fire ready. The boys had a great dinner. It was very cold that night but, the fire kept them warm. The kid finished his cross and told Tom when he gets to Ft. Sumner he's going to put it in the ground at Jake's apple orchard. Tom stored the meat in his cooler. They called it a night and crawled into their sleeping bags. The kid slept next to the wood so he could just grab some and throw it on the fire to keep it going. Morning came and they made some coffee before continuing on their way. A truck was coming down the road and a rancher motioned for Tom to stop. The kid took off his hat so the rancher wouldn't recognize him. The rancher asked Tom what he was doing out there. Tom replied by asking him what he was doing out there. Tom told the rancher that they had been hog hunting on their way to Ft. Sumner. Then he also said that the land was BLM federal open land for anyone and that he knew what his rights were. The rancher didn't say too much to Tom but instead just drove away. Tom and the kid continued on. They came to another old rock house built on a cliff where they decided to set up camp for a couple of days. As they cooked more pork Tom looked at Billy and told him that maybe he really was the kid one hundred and twenty years ago. The kid told Tom that only in death would he ever know why this experience had happened to him. Tom then told Billy that everyone was really going to miss him. "I will miss everyone with all of my heart", said Billy. They agreed that they had some good times.

Tom and Billy stayed in this rock house for days

Tom told Billy that the Pecos River was the hardest river to cross because of it's sandy bottom. The kid really cared a lot for Jake who had done so much for him. Tom told Billy that Jake was a tough son of a buck and not to worry. After a couple of days of camping they continued on their path. It was now December 29, 1991. They were getting closer to Ft. Sumner as they came in from the east.

Billy and his friends would sometimes hike these partially caved pathways

The church between Roswell and Ft. Sumner, NM

They stopped at the cemetery to hang out for a while and decided to set up camp in the park next to it. Later that evening after dinner the kid and Tom walked to the cage where William H. Bonny was buried. The kid told Tom that William H. Bonny was caught by surprise by sheriff Pat Garrett and that he didn't have time to ask for forgiveness for his sins. The kid asked Tom if he believed in God. Tom said yes. The kid told Tom that it is always important to ask for forgiveness for your sins and try to live right. "Nobody's perfect, but if people try to do right this would be a better world to live in", said Billy. After hanging out at the cemetery for a while they went to the park to call it a night. December 30th came and the end was near.

Farmland in the valley in old Ft. Sumner, NM

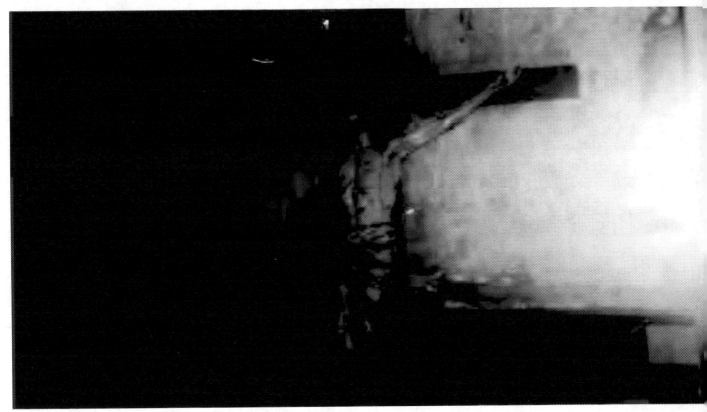
December 31, 1991, Billy pays respect to the Lord

Tom and the kid rode over to Bosque Redondo to set up camp for one more day. Tom went and got more ice to put over the hog meat. Tom told the kid that the time was coming. Billy said "I reckon so". They just walked around exploring Bosque Redondo where the Indians took their long walk. Tom did some target shooting while the kid just relaxed. Soon it was night time and Tom was telling stories by the campfire. Morning came and it was New Year's Eve. The kid looked at Tom and said "Let's get to it". They began heading up to Jake's ranch. Tom and the kid saw Jake as he drove up on a tractor. Jake asked Billy if he had come back to work. The kid told Jake "Not this time". Then Jake asked Billy what he was talking about. "This time I won't be coming back", said the kid as he turned away and started walking toward the apple orchard with his cross in hand. Jake told Billy that he could not leave and never come back. He then told Billy that Ft. Sumner was his home. Billy just kept walking until he was in the orchard. With a tear in his eye the kid grabbed a big rock and began to pound his cross into the ground. Tom asked Billy if he had time to ask for forgiveness for his sins. "Yes, I do", replied Billy. The kid continued pounding the cross into the earth. The wind picked up and the sun began to shine. Billy went over to Tom and Jake and told them that is was good riding with them. The kid then took his bags and other belongings from Jake's. Tom and Billy shook hands and went their separate ways. The kid headed east and disappeared into the sunset never to return to New Mexico.

Lincoln visitors say they've seen a ghost

Billy the Kid? Reincarnated

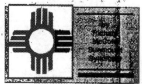

In the summer of 1989, 22-year-old Billy Cox of Bartow, Florida, got a hankering to go west for the first time, looking for adventure.

He got off the Greyhound bus in Roswell and wandered into the local museum. The historian there, Ken Hobbs, took one look at him, gasped, and pronounced him a dead ringer for the most famous outlaw ever to wander through those parts: Billy the Kid.

For Cox, it was the start of something ... well, peculiar.

A few days later Hobbs drove Billy Cox to the town of Lincoln, where the Kid killed several men before he was gunned down at Fort Sumner in 1881 by Sheriff Pat Garrett, at the age of 21.

These events are now memorialized in a state monument, run by Ranger Jack Rigney. "This is Billy the Kid from Florida," Hobbs said to his friend the ranger — and Rigney could not believe his eyes.

Only one authenticated photograph of the Kid is known to exist. In it he wears a crumpled top hat, a low-slung gunbelt and a bandanna, and holds a Winchester rifle by his side. The camera captures his face straight-on. The face is identical to Billy Cox's.

When the ranger caught his breath, he and Cox struck a quick rapport. They stayed in touch after Billy took the bus back home and resumed his work as a busboy in a restaurant. Rigney visited relatives in Florida that winter and stopped by to see Billy, who had rounded

pistol and a Winchester, tourists pointed at him in astonishment.

Then they wanted him to pose for photographs and paid him five or ten dollars without him having to ask. When there was a crowd, he could pick up $30 or $40 at a time.

At daily presentations at the state monument, Rigney would tell the story of Billy the Kid, then ask if anyone believed in ghosts. On cue, Cox would walk in and strike the pose. The tourists would gasp, grab for their cameras — and leave a donation.

In his spare time, Cox tried to do things that the first Billy had done in Lincoln County, more than 100 years ago. He borrowed horses and went riding through open country. He slept out under the stars. He did odd jobs on area ranches. He stopped to chat with everybody in town, and accepted handouts at many houses. He went to saloons in

Truth or Consequences and Taiban, and at Eastern State Fair in Roswell. He won lookalike contests, staged shootouts with "Pat Garrett's Gang," was featured on local television and in national magazines, even had videotape made about him. The pay was always chancy, but enough to keep him canned pork and beans.

But the tourist season finally ended — last October Cox realized things were changing. Rigney, in whose house he had lived summer, started dropping hints about Flori Then the deputy sheriff in Lincoln drove one day and asked him outright: "when going back home, Billy?"

'Outlaws' to dedicate marker

By Don Cooper
CNJ CITY EDITOR

PUERTA DE LUNA — In December 1880, Billy the Kid, wearing leg irons and guarded by Sheriff Pat Garrett, arrived at Alexander "Padre Polaco" Grzelachowski's house.

The legendary outlaw ate his last Christmas meal at Grzelachowski's home, which also served as a stagecoach stop. Less than seven months later, the Kid would be dead — shot to death by ete Maxwell's home near Fort

rmer Polish priest, served in ipating in the 1862 Battle of anta Fe, before he settled in area in 1874.

embers of the Billy the Kid tate officials will gather to marker at the Grzelachowski are expected to begin about

The Kid's alive and selling trees here

Continued from 1B

and people just treat me nice like they treated the Kid back then. People in Fort Sumner hid him out from the sheriff — from Pat Garrett."

Part of Cox's adventure has been the assortment of odd jobs he's taken on to earn his keep.

"I wanted to kinda struggle," he said. "It'd be better that way.

"Doin' odd jobs to help people out — chopping wood, something the Kid woulda done, stack wood, build fences, repair fences, digging post holes. Whatever needs to

Cox

be done. I come into their house and work for them and eat and, like, build a relationship with them."

He also has been taking in sights he believes were in the Kid's line of sight during his roamings, photographing and collecting memories along the way — "seeing the country where he was at, you know."

Similarities between William H. Bonney and William H. Cox

- Their names
- Both are Irish
- Both are Sagittarians
- Each lost his mother while in his teens
- Both were born on the East Coast — Bonney in New York City; Cox in Florida
- Cox is small in stature; so was Bonney
- Similar facial features

While other belongings remain in New Mexico, Cox carries his pictures and other mementos with him in a stack of photo albums, which he willingly displays.

He has no idea whether he's at the beginning, middle or end of the Billy the Kid adventure — "the plan is just work. Keep working, make money" — but Cox says it can't go on forever. The Kid was killed when he was 21; Cox turned 25 yesterday.

"I never thought I'd get of but I'm gettin' older. I don't 25 though, do I? Or 24?"

SHORT TAKES/ STAFF & WIRE REPORTS

'Billy the Kid?'

CNJ Staff Photo: Don Cooper

No, it's not Billy the Kid, though this resident of Fort Sumner could pass for the infamous New Mexico outlaw who was killed in 1881 near the De Baca County town. This modern-day 'Billy' sitting on the steps outside the Fort Sumner Masonic lodge is William H. Cox. Cox was dressed like Billy the Kid as part of Fort Sumner's annual Old Fort Days celebration.

191

Billy the Kid Outlaw Gang

PUERTO DE LUNA–The Billy the Kid Outlaw Gang featuring Billy Cox as Billy the Kid were at the dedication of the Grzelachowski Territorial House Saturday.

Billy the Kid ate his last Christmas dinner at the Grzelachowski house and was a friend to Alexander Grzelachowski.

Billy Cox has won the Billy the Kid look alike contest for three years.

Billy Cox Enjoyed Looking Like Billy The Kid

By JIM KELLY
Of The Herald-Advocate

The Herald-Advocate
Thursday, July 1, 2004

A couple of hundred persons joined in the dedication of the Grzelchowski building in Puerto De Luna as a historical and culture site during ceremonies Saturday.

BILLY THE KID

is alive and well and selling Christmas trees at the corner of Campbell and Grant

BILLY'S LIFE

Continued From Page 1

about the history of Billy the Kid.

He said a historian named Ken Hobbs saw him in the museum in Roswell and told him he looked just like Billy the Kid.

Cox, who has lived off and on in Plant City, said Hobbs and his family took him in and drove him to Lincoln, N.M. He described it as a one-street town with adobe homes on each side of the road. Nestled in the foothills, it had the Rio Bonito flowing behind homes on the north side.

Hobbs and Jack Rigney, a ranger working at the courthouse, both agreed that Cox was a dead ringer, or live ringer, for the Kid. Soon, Cox started to enjoy the role.

He noted that his and the Kid's first names were the same, they both were Irish, both Sagittarians, both lost their mothers when they were in their teens, both were born on the East Coast — Billy the Kid in New York City and Cox in Florida. Both were small in stature and had similar facial features.

The World Book encyclopedia describes Billy the Kid as a cattle thief and killer in New Mexico. He killed as many as 21 people. His real name was Henry McCarty, but after moving to the frontier in 1873, he shot a man to death and took on the name of William H. Bonney, then Billy the Kid.

When a rancher who had befriended him was killed in a frontier feud, the Kid, as a member of a posse called "the Regulators," helped kill the murderers.

He later became a cattle rustler but finally agreed to testify against the other Regulator participants in exchange for a pardon.

Billy Cox returned to Florida in 1991. He now works at Father 'n' Son Quick-Dry Carpet Cleaning in Lakeland.

The World Book encyclopedia describes Billy the Kid as a cattle thief and killer in New Mexico. He killed as many as 21 people.

Fearing that state officials could not protect him from some of the men he planned to testify against, he escaped and reportedly continued his life as a rustler and killer.

After Pat Garrett became Lincoln County sheriff in November 1880, he trapped Billy. Sentenced to be hanged, Billy killed two deputies and escaped from jail April 28, 1881.

The sheriff found the Kid in a house in Fort Sumner, a military post near the town of Fort Sumner, N.M., and killed him July 14, 1881.

Since then, there have been many who claim that someone else was killed and that the real Kid lived under another name until his death years later.

Perhaps the history and intrigue of that long-ago event is what tempted Cox to retrace the Kid's steps across New Mexico, working on ranches, camping out and eventually portraying the Kid in re-enactments.

There came a time, however, when Cox ran into a little difficulty himself. He said he had been portraying the Kid for tourists and appearing in look-alike contests when the tide turned. He said some people thought they should get part of the money he was earning.

Or, as he puts it, "The deputy thought I was getting lost in the character."

Cox felt the time had come in 1991 for him to return to Florida. He planted a cross in the ground in Fort Sumner on a friend's ranch and returned home. He now works at Father 'n' Son Quick-Dry Carpet Cleaning in Lakeland.

As he nears middle age, his resemblance to Kid continues to fade. But he dreams of perhaps seeing his own life in a movie. Because, he said, "It's American history."

Correspondent Punky Snow can be reached at (813) 754-3765.

BILLY THE KID REINCARNATED?

IN THE LATE 80'S & EARLY 90'S WILLIAM H. COX II, WHO WAS BORN & RAISED IN POLK COUNTY, FL, ENDED UP IN LINCOLN COUNTY, NEW MEXICO. THERE HE BECAME KNOWN AS "BILLY THE KID" & AFTER 2 YEARS, ACCORDING TO LEGEND, MYSTERIOUSLY DISAPPEARED FROM FT. SUMNER, NM, ON DECEMBER 31, 1991.

The poster was made of Polk County native William H. Cox II.

The Herald-Advocate

(USPS 578-780)

Thursday, July 1, 2004

You Can't Take 'The Kid' Out Of Billy

LOCAL MAN SPENT YEARS PORTRAYING INFAMOUS CRIMINAL FROM WILD WEST

By PANKY SNOW
Tribune correspondent

PLANT CITY — Think Elvis. Think all the Elvis lookalikes. Think a little chunk of history.

Now, think Billy the Kid and how people like to emulate him just like they copy Elvis.

The original Billy the Kid was killed July 14, 1881, in New Mexico, but a man who once looked like a carbon copy of Billy is living in this area.

His name is William Hope Cox II. And although he was born in Bartow on Dec. 13, 1966, his heart, he said, belongs to another time, another place.

When he walked into The Tampa Tribune's Plant City office last week, he didn't look much like the infamous Billy the Kid, but he talked the talk and walked the walk.

Under his arm was a stack of clippings and pictures that backed up his story. In one of the pictures, he was standing next to an authentic 1879 picture of William H. Bonney, later known as Billy the Kid.

And, yes, they did look alike, that Billy and this area's Billy Cox. Of course, the tall black hat, rumpled appearance and rifle by his side added to the illusion in the picture.

The play-acting all started in 1988 when Cox saw the Western movie "Young Guns." He said he fell in love with the New Mexico scenery and tales of the Old West. His mother had died when he was 14, and Cox said the call of the wild was strong.

He didn't exactly jump on his horse and ride away, but he did take a bus to Roswell, N.M., the next year. There, he visited a museum to learn more

See BILLY'S LIFE, Page 11 ▶

Like infamous Billy, Cox ran into difficulty, too.

Billy Cox, left, shares more than just a name with Billy the Kid. They look alike, are both Sagittarians and both lost their mothers in their teens.

193

It's like the mail route guys, they are so happy when they see him. The lady behind the counter at the bus station. They just dig him all over. If you get introduced by Billy Cox, somebody puts you up. It was like my whole fantasy of getting to run with the Kid. It's as close as it gets. One of Billy's best friends is a guy named Tom. That thing Alan Moore was talking about in his books, how events in history begin to repeat themselves...I just felt like I walked right into that. It was like the best time to come onto the Billy scene. The energy is really right, something is going on that's far beyond our capacity to understand. I wouldn't be at all surprised if it ends up with all of us owning property in Lincoln. Throwing Billy Fests the way Billy Fests should be thrown.

I don't want to get off only into Billy because the whole Lincoln County thing, there's a big picture to it. But he's it. Running with Cox began to give me a whole taste of it, how Billy is the whole crux. I think I've come a lot closer to understanding Billy the Kid than I ever could have sitting in my house in Paterson reading books about it.

Celine: When I did my interview with Cox, at first I thought some of what he said was kind of pretentious — you know, 'If people want to know what it was like to run with the Kid, I can give them the Kid. They can be with me.' But as I see it unfold...he's right.

Bob: That's what I told Bob Hart. He's doing it the right way. Cox is an interesting character, there's an ego to him, too, and there was to the Kid. But he's good natured. I know, I like him, I got close to him really fast.

We ran together, we had some adventures, and that's the weird thing with the Regulators, too. They all had ranches, jobs so they would gather and run a mission, and they'd be together for a few days, risk their lives together, and then they'd split up and go to their ranches until something else happened that brought them together.

The Billy the Kid Outlaw Gang meeting was on the anniversary of his assassination, and I made a drawing for this girl, and I put the date down — I dated it in Ruidoso, and I realized it was a date of his death. And I got this...feeling. Of how things work.

Billy The Kid
Claims District 8 As His Home

Billy the Kid (Billy Cox) recently joined Senator Pete Campos in Puerto de Luna at the old Grzelachowski home for a re-creation of the last Christmas he celebrated.

"Our senatorial district is rich in history. With our people, history and natural resources, we can definitely be proud of San Miguel, Guadalupe, Debaca and Lincoln Counties," Senator Campos said. The Senator did not want to say to much about Billy for fear of retribution!

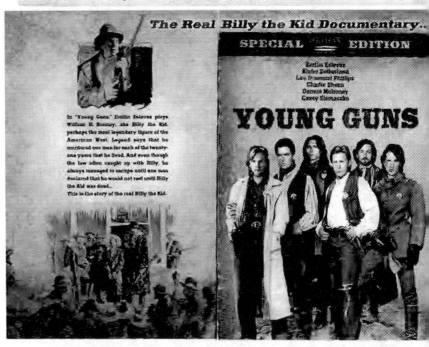

Above: Illustration of William H. Cox II. Photo originally taken by Bob Boze Bell in Lincoln, NM 1990

NEW MEXICO

Left—Cox strikes a pose very similar to this classic photo circa 1879 of William H. Bonney, known as Billy the Kid, above.

Photos on opposite page—William H. Cox II as a youngster always hammed it up for the camera as a cowboy gunslinger. He's shown with the guns and cowboy hat in these photos taken in the early '70s.

THE KID'S DOUBLE BLAZES NEW TRAIL

Over the years there have been many Billy the Kid wannabes. But how many have actually left their homes to pursue that dream in Lincoln?

The story you are about to read is true, the names have not been changed to protect the innocent. It is about a young man, William H. Cox II of Lakeland, Fla., who decided to take on the legacy of Billy the Kid.

Similarities between the two men are interesting. Both were given the name William H., share an Irish heritage, are Sagittarians, lost their mothers as teen-agers, were born on the East Coast, are small in stature and have similar facial features and hair.

Was there a real connection? In early boyhood photos of Billy in Florida, he was always toting a toy gun or posing in a gunfighter-like stance. But not until Billy saw the Western movie Young Guns was he inspired to head out West.

Strolling through a Roswell museum to learn more about the Lincoln County War, he was "discovered" by historian Ken Hobbs. Hobbs was amazed by his uncanny resemblance to the Kid and hauled Billy off to the town of Lincoln itself. Jack Rigney, a ranger who worked at the building known as the Courthouse, was just as surprised as Hobbs. And so it began.

Outfitted with a stovepipe hat and 30-30 Winchester, Billy was ready for his photo shoots and love affair with the public. Being an irascible look-alike celebrity made him particularly popular with the ladies.

Billy had his share of women and a good time during this period. Sadly, all good things must come to an end. Business just wasn't there anymore. To supplement his income, Billy did ranch work, deliveries and pumpkin picking. He even sold Christmas trees in Tucson, Ariz.

After two years William H. Cox II disappeared. But he accomplished quite a bit during his short reign as the Kid. He was the subject of newspaper columns, attended dedications, made public appearances, had his photo in Smithsonian magazine and won three Billy the Kid look-alike contests. It is rumored Billy left a small wooden cross on his friend Jake's ranch in Fort Sumner as a farewell gift to New Mexico.

Billy freely admits that he got run out of Lincoln town. But a dude's got to do what a dude's got to do! And if the tourists hankered after him to pose for pictures, why not accommodate them, accepting the stipends offered? The kind townspeople of Lincoln perhaps felt that this "new" Billy had just overstayed his welcome.

Billy now lives in Bartow, Fla., working in the carpet-cleaning business with his dad. But if you need the Kid for an event, Billy is available. Plus he'll give you a darn good deal on your carpets! He can be reached at (863) 533-6118. Or check the Web site at www.FatherNSon.QuickDry.00Home.com.

If you ever find yourself driving among the juniper-clad hills along the "lovelorn trail" and your eye catches a glimpse of a figure on horseback in the distance, let your imagination take over. Could it be Billy the Kid or is it William H. Cox II, heading to one of the parties to find a little love and female companionship? Whoever it is, chances are he'll be warmly welcomed.
—Carol Kay

Article courtesy of New Mexico Magazine

195

THE LAND OF ENCHANTMENT

AND AT THE FORT

FORT SUMNER PRIDE

Tanya Armstrong

THE OUTLAW GANG
ON THE LOOKOUT FOR BILLY

BY PAMELA BAMERT
PHOTOGRAPHY BY RUSSELL BAMERT

196

BILLY THE KID
In Real Life: William "Billy" Cox

Billy Cox is a certified member of the Billy the Kid Outlaw Gang and was back with us at the 2000 BTK campout, along with some of his gang members from Florida.

A bit of history on one William H. Cox, alias Billy the Kid. He often portrayed the Kid in reinactments in New Mexico, from Puerto de Luna to Old Fort Sumner to Lincoln and beyond. He was a stand-in for many of Bob Boze Bell's scenes featured in his two volumes of THE ILLUSTRATED LIFE AND TIMES OF BILLY THE KID. And, did I say he was from Florida?

Back in the late 1980s and early 1990s Billy Cox the Kid wandered around New Mexico retracing the Kid's steps, working on ranches and camping out where the Kid possibly stayed over 120 years ago. He called the experience his "adventure" and got caught up in the mystique of Billy's life. And he lived that life for a while. Lot of people still believe he is really Billy the Kid!

Even his "Gang" in Florida believes. Won't tell you where they are hid out for that would be giving away classified secrets. This Editor is taking a big chance that some one will recognize thier locale in Florida from the photo present here, and if so, they will have to pack up and leave for a better climate, like Old Mexico!

The names of the members of his gang in the photos are aliases, to protect the guilty.

Standing inside the remains of the faint rock foundation of the shack, Joe Bowlin describes how Billy became trapped. He points across the undulating grassland and traces the route Garrett and his men traveled to sneak up on the Kid. "When you stand here, you know you're where Billy the Kid once stood. To me, that's just electrifying," he says with a shiver.

What Bowlin terms electrifying, William Cox, who bears an uncanny resemblance to Billy the Kid, calls "cool" or "bad." Like many young adults, Cox, 25, is caught up in the mystique of Billy's life, thanks to a little help from Hollywood. It seems each generation is presented a different view of Billy's life on film, and the popular Young Guns and Young Guns II have revived an interest for Cox and others in search of a hero.

Granted, Cox, a native of Florida who has been wandering around New Mexico retracing Billy's steps, working on ranches and camping out where the Kid probably stayed a century ago, takes the attraction further than most. He calls the experience his "adventure" and believes he has gained from it some insight into the outlaw's character. "He was just a kid," he says simply and adds that Billy was probably somewhat of a media creation; he offers a conclusion similar to what some historians have drawn.

Cox often portrays the Kid in re-enactments the Gang regularly stages at historic locations. The most recent re-creation was at Puerto de Luna, where Billy ate his last Christmas meal after being captured at Stinking Springs.

re-enactment of the killing of the Kid is
aged in the Abreu house, which is a dupli-
te of the Pete Maxwell house in Fort
umner. Billy's character calls out " ¿Quien
, quien es?" when he senses the presence
another person.

On the Desert
The return of Billy The Kid

David Eppele

There's only one authenticated photograph of Billy The Kid known to exist. That's the old tintype photo where Billy wears an old crumpled top hat, has a gun belt slung low on his hip and holds a Winchester rifle by his side.

Billy looks just like a baby-faced teen-ager imitating some desperado. It's truly hard to believe that he had some serious character disorders ... he liked to steal things and he liked to shoot ... people! Billy The Kid died at age 21, having killed 21 men during his gun-slinging career.

Arizona Cactus member Armando Jaramillo, of Las Cruces, N.M., recently shot me a Polaroid photo he took last summer when he and his wife, Clorinda, were visiting relatives in Lincoln, N.M.

The relatives asked "Mando" and Clorinda if they had been to the New Mexico State Monument in Lincoln.

Mando said: "Yeah, we were there the day they opened the monument and we've seen it a couple of times since then ... it's OK. But if I had to give it a grade, it would have to be a C-minus."

"Well cousin," says the other cousin, "You'd better get over there by 2 o'clock today because Ranger Rigney is going to put on a show that you just won't believe!" Mando said his Primo (cousin) reminded him to take his camera.

At two that afternoon, Mando and Clorinda were part of a small audience of 20 who began listening to Ranger Jack Rigney tell the story of the life of New Mexico's most famous person, Billy The Kid. Ranger Rigney traced Billy from the east to Lincoln County and points in-between.

The ranger had done his homework ... he knew as much about Billy The Kid as any living historian could know.

When Ranger Rigney got to the part where Billy The Kid gets plugged by Sheriff Pat Garrett, Mando says he was ready to leave. "Eeejo, the way they present that stuff ... why it's worse than the history class I slept through in high school!"

Little did he know that Ranger Rigney was setting him up!

Ranger Rigney drones on and on ... says that even to this day, people report seeing "someone in an old, crushed top hat walking out in the pastures, or riding up in the forest above town."

Then the ranger asks a silly question of his audience. He asks them if they believe in ghosts.

Mando said he was "todo shookado" (all shook-up) when a perfect double for Billy The Kid casually strode into the mu-

seum and struck the exact pose seen in the old 1880 photo! Mando said there was a stampede as the audience clambered to get a photograph of this double for Billy The Kid.

"I asked Clorinda to get some shots with the 35mm. while I managed to work my way up close for some Polaroid shots."

Mando said that just about everyone in the audience dropped a $10 or a $20 in the donation box in payment for this "photo opportunity."

Mando enclosed a Polaroid print of 22-year-old Billy Cox, of Bartow, Fla.

As I write, I am looking at a Polaroid shot that shows Billy Cox staring straight into the camera ... that young, innocent face, those cold, cold eyes!

Mando says that the residents of Lincoln got nervous while Billy Cox was running around town, packing an unloaded pistol and Winchester rifle. "This guy was knocking down anywhere from $60 to $200 a day, pretending to be Billy The Kid. And they ran him out of town because some Deputy Sheriff was worried that Mr. Cox would get 'lost in his character!'"

"Heck," writes Mando, "I think they should bring him back and use him even more! Now that I think back, the show that Ranger Rigney presented was great.

I think Ranger Rigney should be promoted to the director of tourism for the state of New Mexico!

Visit the Arizona Cactus Web site at http://www.arizonacactus.com.

WORTLEY HOTEL
Bill of Fare

LUNCH

SALADS
DINNER SALAD
CHEF'S SALAD

SANDWICHES
HAMBURGER
CHEESEBURGER
WITH GREEN CHILE
GRILLED CHEESE
CHICKEN BREAST
FRENCH DIP
WORTLEY DELUXE
STACKED ROAST BEEF, CHEESE, GREEN CHILE STRIP

SIDE ORDERS
FRENCH FRIES
COLE SLAW

DESSERTS
COBBLER
A LA MODE

BEVERAGES
COFFEE, TEA OR LEMONADE

Joe Bowlin and William "Billy the Kid" Cox

Photos that were used in Bob Boze Bell's
book "The Illustrated Life and Times of Billy
the Kid". Photos courtesy of Bob Boze Bell.

Photos that were used in Bob Boze Bell's book "The Illustrated Life and Times of Billy the Kid". Photos courtesy of Bob Boze Bell.

199

Photo that was used in Bob Boze Bell's book "The Illustrated Life and Times of Billy the Kid".
Photo courtesy of Bob Boze Bell.

I would like to thank God for giving me life when I didn't have a life at all. There was only darkness. I would also like to thank the following people:

Uncle John
John
Matt ,Brad, Ricky and Junior for your loyalty and the good times during high school and after.
William Sr.
Allison
Terry for the tennis interviews
Jose and the Lakeland gang
Chris
Panky from the Tampa Tribune
Jim from the Wauchula Advocate
Joyce from the Ft. Meade Leader
Citizens of New Mexico
Ken
Donna
Brian
Dennis
Mathew
Tom
Jack
Manny
Darla
Harvey
Dustin
Tim and wife
Rob
Sharon
Kevin
Jake-Sharon's father
Joe
Colleen
Dora
Lacy
Patrick
Blake
Leroy
Robert
Roy
Bob Boze Bell
Bob

(continues on pg. 202)

Scott
Bobby
Billy and his family
Eddie
Sammy
Eric
New Jersey Bob
Bonnie
Billy The Kid Outlaw Gang
Joe
Marilyn
Don
Joe
 Carolyn
James
Billy-AZ
Gary
Johnny
Jennifer
Maureen
Crystal
Eddie G.
Stan
Buck
Darrell
Jake and Leona
David
Alan
Kenneth
Big Bill
Victor
Harold
Joe
Staff of New Mexico Magazine
Emily
Pamela
Russell
Carol

A special thanks to the most talented musician that ever played, Prince. He is a true inspiration to live life to the ultimate.

Here's to the old school.

A special thanks to the following towns of New Mexico:

Lincoln
Ft. Sumner
Puerto de Luna
Roswell
Carrizozo
White Oaks
Capitan
Capitan Peak
Guadeloupe
Santa Rosa
Ruidoso
Nogal
Cedar Creek
Other surrounding areas
ALL OF IT

Also, I would like to thank the cast, crew and makers of the movie Young Guns for the inspiration they gave me to find the truth.

I would like to thank everyone listed for the good times and memories and to them for not putting money or the system first. Thanks for putting friendship first. That's what's really important in life. It's not what you do with money but, what you can do without it. It can lead you to the truth.

TRUE POWER

"Dont be ordinary, be original", William Cox II

"Last but not least I would like to thank my beautiful wife Shaunda Cox for her efforts in helping me to complete my book. Thank you for standing by me and being so supportive. I love you always and forever"- William Cox II.

Author: W.H.C II

Photo on back of book: William H. Cox II in Guadalupe, New Mexico